Workbook

Working

Fifth Edition

Larry J. Bailey

SOUTH-WESTERN
CENGAGE Learning

Australia • Brazil • Japan • Korea • Mexico • Singapore • Spain • United Kingdom • United States

ISBN-13: 978-1-111-43022-1
ISBN-10: 1-111-43022-5

South-Western Cengage Learning
5191 Natorp Boulevard
Mason, OH 45040
USA

Cengage Learning is a leading provider of customized learning solutions with office locations around the globe, including Singapore, the United Kingdom, Australia, Mexico, Brazil, and Japan. Locate your local office at:
international.cengage.com/region.

Cengage Learning products are represented in Canada by Nelson Education, Ltd.

For your course and learning solutions, visit
www.cengage.com/school.

Visit our company website at
www.cengage.com.

Printed in the United States of America
2 3 4 5 6 7   17 16 15 14

CONTENTS

Contents   v

             Contents

Contents   vii

Part 1 ACTIVITIES

The activities that follow were developed to accompany the textbook *Working, 5E*. A total of 135 activities are included relating to the 22 textbook chapters. They provide opportunities for you to practice and apply concepts and skills introduced in the textbook.

A wide variety of problems, forms, rating scales, completion exercises, puzzles, and other approaches are used to make learning relevant and interesting. Some activities depend on use of the textbook. Others require you to use library or Internet reference materials or to collect information outside the school. A balance of individual- and group-oriented activities is provided. Most activities can be completed as part of a normal class period. A few activities, however, may require several days to complete.

In addition to reinforcing chapter objectives, these activities require you to apply communication, math and measurement, problem solving, and many other academic and employability skills. Some activities and exercises such as test-type items and math problems have only one correct answer. Many others, though, ask you to provide your own opinions and points of view. Do so. Think about the question and analyze the situation carefully before coming to a conclusion. Join with your classmates in follow-up discussion of the activities.

Work experience education has a very clear purpose: to help you obtain employment and succeed and progress on the job. The activities in this workbook can help you further develop the skills needed to progress toward a successful and satisfying career.

Chapter 1   Learn About Work

1-1   Why People Work

1-2   Get Self-Information

1-3   Understand Industries and Occupations

1-4   Investigate Occupations

Activity 1-1 Why People Work

Select three employed individuals of different ages, sexes, and occupations. Show them the seven statements that follow. Have them rank the statements on scrap paper from most important (1) to least important (7). Then insert the rankings in this form. Combine the data with those of your classmates to compute an average for all the rankings. Complete the form and make a graph or chart of the results.

Reasons to Work	1	2	3	Average
■ Earn money	_______	_______	_______	_______
■ Be around people	_______	_______	_______	_______
■ It is satisfying and makes me feel good about myself.	_______	_______	_______	_______
■ Because people look up to me	_______	_______	_______	_______
■ To learn and grow	_______	_______	_______	_______
■ Makes me feel good physically	_______	_______	_______	_______
■ Allows me to express my interests and abilities	_______	_______	_______	_______

Study these data. What similarities and differences do you observe?

____

____

____

____

How do **your** reasons for wanting a job compare with the average rankings? _____________

____

____

____

____

Chapter 1 Learn About Work

Activity 1-2 Occupations and Jobs, I

A person having an occupation can work at many different types of jobs. For each occupation listed, identify three examples of different jobs where an individual could possibly work.

Auto mechanic
____

____

____

Bookkeeper
____

____

Child-care worker
____

____

Data entry worker
____

____

Dietitian
____

____

Drafter
____

____

Clinical
laboratory technician
____

____

Receptionist
____

____

Chapter 1 Learn About Work

Activity 1-3 Occupations and Jobs, II

In the previous activity, you were asked to provide examples to illustrate how "a person having an occupation can work at many different types of jobs." Four additional characteristics about the relationship between occupations and jobs are stated below. Read each statement, study the example, and then complete the exercise.

1. A person may change jobs but keep the same occupation. For example, Ron was a welder at Deepwater Ship Building Company who left his job to work as a welder for High-Rise Construction Company. Provide another example of this relationship.

   ____

   ____

   ____

2. A person may change occupations but keep the same job. For example, Lu-yin was a cashier at Town and Country Food Store. When the store expanded, Lu-yin was promoted to Assistant Store Manager. Provide another example of this relationship.

   ____

   ____

   ____

3. A person may change both occupation and job. Gary was a medical laboratory technician at Metropolitan Hospital. He left this job to become a health occupations instructor at Lakeland Community College. Provide another example of this relationship.

   ____

   ____

   ____

4. Persons having the same occupation may perform different duties on the job. For example, Tanya, who is a retail sales worker at Nadia's Dress Shop, spends most of her time at the cash register ringing up sales and bagging purchases. Lenoir, also a retail sales worker at Nadia's, spends most of her time assisting customers in the fitting room and marking garments for alterations. Provide another example of this relationship.

   ____

   ____

   ____

Chapter 1 Learn About Work

Activity 1-4 Rating Interests

Listed below and on the next four pages are a number of work activities found in a broad range of industries and occupations. Show whether you would like doing each activity by circling one of the three choices as follows:

L = I would like this activity
? = I am not certain whether I would like or dislike it.
D = I would not like this activity.

You may circle the **L** even if you do not have training for or experience in an activity. Circle the **?** only when you cannot decide whether you would like or dislike an activity or when you do not know what the activity is.

CAREER CLUSTER 1

Develop new food items for production	L	?	D
Study basic principles of plant and animal life	L	?	D
Implement soil and water management techniques	L	?	D
Manage a farm for another owner	L	?	D
Catch and gather fish or other aquatic animals	L	?	D
Plant tree seedlings	L	?	D
Harvest trees for lumber and pulp	L	?	D
Inspect and grade lumber	L	?	D
Investigate and report on accidents affecting the environment.	L	?	D
Oversee maintenance of farm equipment	L	?	D

CAREER CLUSTER 2

Prepare architectural designs and construction drawings	L	?	D
Build houses and other small buildings	L	?	D
Install and finish drywall and plaster	L	?	D
Build forms, pour, and finish concrete	L	?	D
Prepare and maintain maps and descriptions of land surveys	L	?	D
Install electric wiring	L	?	D
Paint and paper walls	L	?	D
Install and repair plumbing and fixtures	L	?	D
Fabricate and install sheet metal objects	L	?	D
Construct bridges, towers, and structural metal frameworks	L	?	D

(Continued on next page)

Chapter 1 Learn About Work

CAREER CLUSTER 3

Write articles and short stories	L	?	D
Edit work of other writers	L	?	D
Control audio equipment during radio and television broadcasts	L	?	D
Design fabrics or fashions	L	?	D
Paint or sketch pictures	L	?	D
Photograph people, places, and events	L	?	D
Direct plays and theatrical performances	L	?	D
Play a musical instrument or sing as a performance artist	L	?	D
Perform a dance routine	L	?	D
Plan publicity for an organization	L	?	D

CAREER CLUSTER 4

Direct activities for a large company or department	L	?	D
Place phone calls and arrange conference calls	L	?	D
Prepare cost and expenditure statements	L	?	D
Record data and maintain personnel records	L	?	D
Operate office machines	L	?	D
Greet persons and direct them to specific locations	L	?	D
Perform general office duties	L	?	D
Prepare invoices, reports, letters, email, and other documents	L	?	D
Direct human resource plans and activities	L	?	D
Compute product totals and charges for shipments	L	?	D

CAREER CLUSTER 5

Counsel students with educational or behavioral problems	L	?	D
Manage and coordinate an educational district or department	L	?	D
Teach in an elementary or secondary school	L	?	D
Help users locate library materials	L	?	D
Design and produce curriculum materials	L	?	D
Teach children with special needs	L	?	D
Administer and interpret personality tests	L	?	D
Help patrons use computers and other electronic devices	L	?	D
Conduct research and write articles and books	L	?	D
Maintain a collection of historical documents	L	?	D

CAREER CLUSTER 6

Compute taxes owed and prepare tax returns	L	?	D
Estimate home and property values	L	?	D
Operate computers programmed with accounting software	L	?	D
Record and document stock purchases	L	?	D
Assist clients in making financial investments	L	?	D
Analyze and make recommendations regarding loan applications	L	?	D
Locate and monitor overdue accounts	L	?	D
Cash checks and pay out money	L	?	D
Prepare and verify financial reports	L	?	D
Develop a budget for an organization	L	?	D

(Continued on next page)

Chapter 1 Learn About Work

CAREER CLUSTER 7

Conduct research on economic issues   L   ?   D

Interview applicants for public assistance   L   ?   D

Lead combat soldiers into battle   L   ?   D

Plan and coordinate a community survey   L   ?   D

Receive and respond to emergency fire, police, and ambulance calls   L   ?   D

Sort and deliver mail   L   ?   D

Forecast political, economic, and social trends   L   ?   D

Confer with taxpayers to resolve tax return problems   L   ?   D

Make recommendations regarding housing, transportation, zoning, and land use   L   ?   D

Fly combat aircraft   L   ?   D

CAREER CLUSTER 8

Diagnose and treat vision problems   L   ?   D

Provide medical exams and treat ill patients   L   ?   D

Care for pets and sick animals   L   ?   D

Dispense prescription drugs   L   ?   D

Provide physical therapy to an accident victim   L   ?   D

Administer speech and hearing tests   L   ?   D

Conduct medical laboratory tests   L   ?   D

Assist surgeons in an operating room   L   ?   D

Take medical x-rays   L   ?   D

Provide hospital nursing care   L   ?   D

CAREER CLUSTER 9

Plan and develop recipes and menus   L   ?   D

Greet, register, and assign rooms to hotel or motel guests   L   ?   D

Help clients plan travel and lodging accommodations   L   ?   D

Grill, cook, and prepare food for customers   L   ?   D

Coordinate front office activities of hotels and motels   L   ?   D

Work in and monitor an area on a casino floor   L   ?   D

Take orders and serve food and beverages   L   ?   D

Coordinate services for meetings, conferences, conventions, and other events   L   ?   D

Patrol facilities to prevent theft and maintain security   L   ?   D

Organize and lead recreational activities   L   ?   D

CAREER CLUSTER 10

Cut and style hair   L   ?   D

Observe and monitor children's play activities   L   ?   D

Lead participants in physical fitness classes   L   ?   D

Develop and present health-education programs   L   ?   D

Provide skin care and other cosmetic treatments   L   ?   D

Conduct background investigations of individuals   L   ?   D

Consult with families and arrange funerals   L   ?   D

Counsel clients in dealing with substance abuse, mental and physical illness, poverty, and related problems   L   ?   D

Groom and care for household animals   L   ?   D

Supervise group activities of institutional residents   L   ?   D

(Continued on next page)

CAREER CLUSTER 11

Manage computer backup, security, and user help systems	L	?	D
Administer and maintain computer networks	L	?	D
Operate computers and peripheral equipment	L	?	D
Develop solutions involving computer hardware and software	L	?	D
Write, update, and maintain computer programs	L	?	D
Install and maintain computer hardware and software	L	?	D
Confer with clients regarding their information processing or computer needs	L	?	D
Enter data into a computer in the required format	L	?	D
Operate desktop publishing software	L	?	D
Supervise the work of computer programmers, technologists, and technicians	L	?	D

CAREER CLUSTER 12

Guard prisoners in a correctional facility	L	?	D
Record and transcribe court proceedings	L	?	D
Fight fires in homes and buildings	L	?	D
Preside over trials and hearings in a court of law	L	?	D
Represent clients in court or before government agencies	L	?	D
Investigate fire sites and collect evidence	L	?	D
Assist lawyers in the preparation of legal documents and briefs	L	?	D
Enforce motor vehicle and criminal laws	L	?	D
Investigate burglaries and other crimes	L	?	D
Supervise law violators on probation	L	?	D

CAREER CLUSTER 13

Assemble manufactured products in a factory	L	?	D
Repair and paint auto bodies	L	?	D
Set up and operate machine tools	L	?	D
Repair and maintain electronic equipment and appliances	L	?	D
Operate woodworking equipment	L	?	D
Install and repair industrial machinery	L	?	D
Cut and weld metals	L	?	D
Grind and finish eyeglass lenses	L	?	D
Operate electric power generating equipment	L	?	D
Service and repair autos and trucks	L	?	D

CAREER CLUSTER 14

Sell or solicit advertising	L	?	D
Receive and distribute money in retail establishments	L	?	D
Appraise auto damage to determine repair costs	L	?	D
Handle and resolve customer complaints	L	?	D
Sell various types of insurance	L	?	D
Receive and process incoming orders for materials, merchandise, or services	L	?	D
Purchase materials, products, and services for a business	L	?	D
Sell various types of goods and merchandise to retail customers	L	?	D
Authorize credit charges against customers' accounts	L	?	D
Represent and sell products for wholesalers or manufacturers	L	?	D

Chapter 1 Learn About Work

CAREER CLUSTER 15

Analyze statistical information to estimate accident rates	L	?	D
Develop and use weather forecasting tools	L	?	D
Study the chemical properties of materials	L	?	D
Manage biofuels development projects	L	?	D
Assist engineers in various types of R&D projects	L	?	D
Apply math theories and methods to practical problems	L	?	D
Study and analyze information about alternative courses of action	L	?	D
Perform engineering duties	L	?	D
Design computer simulations	L	?	D
Assist scientists to operate, lab equipment	L	?	D

CAREER CLUSTER 16

Control air traffic on and within vicinity of airport	L	?	D
Pilot and navigate aircraft	L	?	D
Arrange transport of goods with shipping or freight companies	L	?	D
Schedule or dispatch workers or service vehicles to appropriate locations	L	?	D
Provide services to airline passengers during flight	L	?	D
Drive trucks or buses	L	?	D
Operate and maintain ships and boats	L	?	D
Prepare items for shipment and maintain shipping records	L	?	D
Operate trains, subways, and streetcars	L	?	D
Make and confirm reservations for transportation or lodging	L	?	D

Interpret your ratings by adding up the number of **L**'s that are circled within each cluster. Place the totals in the spaces to the right of the cluster descriptions.

Cluster Descriptions	**Total**
1. AGRICULTURE, FOOD & NATURAL RESOURCES. Interest in the production and marketing of agricultural commodities and natural resources, the study of plant and animal life, and the preservation and restoration of natural resources.	________
2. ARCHITECTURE & CONSTRUCTION. Interest in planning, designing, constructing, and maintaining homes, buildings, and other person made structures.	________
3. ARTS, A/V TECHNOLOGY & COMMUNICATION. Interest in designing, producing, and publishing various types of media; designing and producing art, fashions, graphics, and other designs; and producing and performing music, dance, and theatre.	________
4. BUSINESS, MANAGEMENT & ADMINISTRATION. Interest in planning, organizing, and conducting business functions essential to efficient and productive business operations from top management through administrative support staff.	________

(Continued on next page)

Chapter 1 Learn About Work

<table>
<tr><td>Cluster Descriptions</td><td>Total</td></tr>
</table>

5. EDUCATION & TRAINING. Interest in managing and providing education and training services, instructional support services, counseling, and library services. ________

6. FINANCE. Interest in providing services related to accounting, banking, insurance, real estate, and investing. ________

7. GOVERNMENT & PUBLIC ADMINISTRATION. Interest in carrying out governmental functions at the local, state, and federal levels, including national defense. ________

8. HEALTH SCIENCE. Interest in diagnosing and treating illness and disease, providing direct patient care, providing technical and administrative support services, promoting wellness, providing rehabilitation services, and conducting medical research. ________

9. HOSPITALITY & TOURISM. Interest in the management, marketing and operations of restaurants and other foodservices, lodging and recreational attractions and events, and travel related services. ________

10. HUMAN SERVICES. Interest in providing personal and social services to children, adults, and families, including animal care. ________

11. INFORMATION TECHNOLOGY. Interest in operating computers and using applications software, managing computer systems and networks, developing computer software, and solving computer hardware and software problems. ________

12. LAW, PUBLIC SAFETY, CORRECTIONS & SECURITY. Interest in providing legal, public safety and security, and protective services, including professional and technical support services. ________

13. MANUFACTURING. Interest in the production of components and assembly of manufactured products and the repair and maintenance of equipment, plants, machines, home appliances, and vehicles. ________

14. MARKETING, SALES & SERVICE. Interest in planning, managing, and performing marketing activities for individuals and businesses, including essential support and service functions. ________

15. SCIENCE, TECHNOLOGY, ENGINEERING & MATHEMATICS. Interest in planning and conducting basic and applied research, applying science and math theories to solution of technical problems, performing engineering duties, and providing technical support to scientists, mathematicians, and engineers. ________

16. TRANSPORTATION, DISTRIBUTION & LOGISTICS. Interest in planning, management, and movement of people, materials, and goods by road, rail, air, water and pipeline, including necessary support services. ________

For which group did you have the highest total? ____

(Continued on next page)

Chapter 1 Learn About Work

Now, turn to Part 2 of this workbook and read about the nature of work performed within your preferred cluster. Read the short occupational descriptions and list below the five occupations in which you are most interested.

____

____

____

____

____

Chapter 1 Learn About Work

Activity 1-5 Rating Aptitudes

Aptitudes are natural talents or developed abilities. For each aptitude listed, rate yourself in terms of whether you have a *low*, *average*, or *high* degree of that aptitude. Circle the appropriate number.

VERBAL	<u>Low</u>		Average		<u>High</u>
■ Ability to express yourself in writing	1	2	3	4	5
■ Ability to talk before a group	1	2	3	4	5
■ Ability to understand the meaning of words	1	2	3	4	5
■ Ability to understand what you have read	1	2	3	4	5

NUMERICAL					
■ Ability to perform math quickly and accurately	1	2	3	4	5
■ Ability to solve math story problems	1	2	3	4	5
■ Ability to analyze and interpret a large amount of data	1	2	3	4	5
■ Ability to work with math formulas and symbols	1	2	3	4	5

CLERICAL SPEED AND ACCURACY					
■ Ability to find important information in written materials and tables	1	2	3	4	5
■ Ability to see differences in written materials	1	2	3	4	5
■ Ability to proofread words and numbers	1	2	3	4	5
■ Ability to record numerical data correctly	1	2	3	4	5

MANUAL DEXTERITY					
■ Ability to coordinate eyes and hands quickly and accurately	1	2	3	4	5
■ Ability to react quickly	1	2	3	4	5
■ Ability to manipulate small objects with the fingers	1	2	3	4	5
■ Ability to work with the hands in placing and turning motions	1	2	3	4	5

(Continued on next page)

MECHANICAL REASONING

	Low		Average		High

- Ability to understand how tools and machines operate 1 2 3 4 5
- Ability to understand how wheels, gears, and pulleys transform motion and energy 1 2 3 4 5
- Ability to understand the practical meaning of differences in weight, size, shape, volume, and balance 1 2 3 4 5
- Ability to select the more efficient of two different methods of performing work 1 2 3 4 5

SPATIAL VISUALIZATION

- Ability to visualize geometric forms in your mind 1 2 3 4 5
- Ability to visualize what a three-dimensional object looks like in two dimensions 1 2 3 4 5
- Ability to visually recognize changes resulting from changing the position of a three-dimensional object 1 2 3 4 5
- Ability to visualize hidden surfaces of a three-dimensional object 1 2 3 4 5

Interpret your ratings. For which two types of aptitudes do you have the highest ratings?

____

Name five different occupations for which your two highest aptitudes would be important.

____

____

Turn to Part 2 of this workbook and read the descriptions for the above occupations. Do the occupations relate to your highest-rated aptitudes? Explain.

____

____

____

____

                                   Chapter 1 Learn About Work

Activity 1-6 Rating Work Values

Read each statement and decide how important it is in choosing the type of work you would like to do. Rate the statements as follows:

3 = Very important
2 = Important
1 = Unimportant

1. Planning your own activities _____
2. Not getting laid off _____
3. Helping other people _____
4. Doing a job well _____
5. Having a good place to work _____
6. Doing a variety of things _____
7. Creating something new _____
8. Having others look up to you _____
9. Being around nice people _____
10. Getting big raises _____
11. Making a contribution to society _____
12. Being your own boss _____
13. Doing different things _____
14. Earning an above-average income _____

15. Knowing your job is permanent _____
16. Trying out a new idea _____
17. Admiring something you have done _____
18. Having pleasant surroundings _____
19. Doing a good deed _____
20. Earning enough to live well _____
21. Creating a better way of doing something _____
22. Deciding things yourself _____
23. Seeing your name in print _____
24. Being able to count on having a job _____
25. Having a varied schedule _____
26. Feeling good about your work _____
27. Being recognized in your field _____

Referring to the chart on the next page, interpret your ratings by adding the numbers together for each type of work value. As an example, for altruism, add together your ratings for Items 3, 11, and 19. Place the number in the chart.

(Continued on next page)

Work Value	Items	Score	Work Score	Items	Score
Altruism	3, 11, 19	_______	Prestige	8, 23, 27	_______
Creativity	7, 16, 21	_______	Earnings	10, 14, 20	_______
Achievement	4, 17, 26	_______	Security	2, 15, 24	_______
Independence	1, 12, 22	_______	Surroundings	5, 9, 18	_______
			Variety	6, 13, 25	_______

What are your three highest-rated work values?

_________________________   _________________________   _________________________

Summarize what your ratings reveal in terms of what is important to you regarding work.

____

____

____

____

Name five occupations that you believe are related to your highest-rated work values.

_________________________   _________________________   _________________________

_________________________   _________________________   _________________________

Turn to Part 2 of this workbook and read the descriptions for the above occupations. Do the occupations relate to your highest-rated work values? Explain.

____

____

____

____

____

Chapter 1 Learn About Work

Activity 1-7 Learning About Your Self

1. Explain what is meant by the following sentence from your text: "Before you select an occupation, you should first answer the question, 'Who am I?'"

    ____

    ____

2. Explain how the following types of self-information can assist you in making occupational decisions.

    Interests: ____

    ____

    ____

    Aptitudes: ____

    ____

    ____

    Work values: ____

    ____

    ____

3. When your work experience job ends, will you seek a job in the same occupation? Explain your answer in relation to what you have learned about your self.

    ____

    ____

4. A job is only a part of life. Describe what you can do in your life to express interests, aptitudes, and work values not being met on the job.

    ____

    ____

    ____

Chapter 1 Learn About Work

Activity 1-8 Reading Tables and Charts

Understanding labor market information requires the ability to read tables and charts. Look up the figures in your textbook as directed and answer the following questions.

Employment Changes by Industry. Refer to Figure 1-7 (page 19 of your textbook).

1. Of the fourteen industries, how many are expected to grow through the year 2018? _____

2. Which industry will grow the most? ____

3. How many industries are expected to decline through the year 2018? ______________

4. By how many thousand jobs will Natural Resources & Mining and Manufacturing decline?

   __________   __________

5. By how many thousand jobs will employment for the following industries change from 2008 to 2018?

   a. Information ________   b. State & Local Gov. ________   c. Construction __________

Fastest-Growing Occupations. Refer to Figure 1-9 (page 20 of your textbook).

6. How many of the 20 fastest-growing occupations are related to health care, medical research, and services for the elderly ? _____

7. How many are computer-related? ____

8. Between 2008 and 2018, what will be the growth rate for the following occupations?

   a. Medical assistants _____%   b. Dental hygienists _____%

   c. Financial examiners _____%

9. What type of education and training is required for the majority of occupations shown in

   Figure 1-9? _______________________________

Occupations with Largest Numerical Increases. Refer to Figure 1-10 (page 21 of your textbook).

10. Between 2008 and 2018, how many new jobs will be added for the following occupations?

    a. Registered nurses __________   b. Retail Salesperson __________

    c. Truck drivers __________

11. Three occupations in Figure 1-9 are also included in Figure 1-10. Name them:

    ________________________________   ________________________________

    ____

12. What type of education and training is required for the majority of occupations shown in

    Figure 1-10? _______________________________

                                    Chapter 1 Learn About Work

Activity 1-9 Exploring Career Clusters

Exploring a career cluster can help you to discover occupations that you are not aware of or have not thought much about. Turn to Part 2 of this workbook and review the list of 16 career clusters. Select one of the clusters to explore. Find information about the cluster in Part 2 and answer the following questions.

Career Cluster: ____

1. Occupations are classified into the 16 clusters on the basis of the type of work performed. What type of work do people in this cluster perform?

____

____

2. In what types of industries (places of employment) are you most likely to find workers from this career cluster?

____

____

____

3. What types of aptitudes are most needed by people who work in this career cluster? (You may wish to review Activity 1-5.)

____

____

____

4. What opportunities does this career cluster seem to offer in terms of allowing you to satisfy your work values? (You may wish to review your work values in Activity 1-6.)

____

____

____

5. Name from one to five occupations found in this career cluster that you would like to learn more about.

_______________________   _______________________   _______________________

_______________________   _______________________   _______________________

Chapter 1 Learn About Work

Activity 1-10 Using the *Occupational Outlook Handbook*

This activity will help you learn how to use the *OOH* effectively to conduct an occupational search. Turn to pages 189–247 of this workbook and answer the following questions.

1. In the online *OOH* (*www.bls.gov/ooh*), what is the best way to find information on occupational groupings?

   ____

2. In the online *OOH*, what are two ways to find information on specific occupations?

   _________________________________   _________________________________

3. In the online *OOH*, where could you read about forces likely to determine employment opportunities and projections for various industries and occupations?

   ____

   ____

The box on the right below lists five of the primary parts of an *OOH* occupational profile. Match the information in the left column with the section where the information can be found.

_________   4. Specialties within the occupation

_________   5. Typical on-the-job training

_________   6. Top and bottom 10% earnings level

_________   7. Projected change in employment

_________   8. Working conditions

_________   9. Definition of the occupation

_________   10. Work experience (if relevant)

_________   11. Technological change

_________   12. Typical duties

_________   13. Entry-level education requirements

_________   14. Work schedules

_________   15. Qualities helpful in performing the work

_________   16. Duties in different industries

_________   17. Industry growth or decline

_________   18. Median annual or hourly wages

_________   19. Industries where employed

_________   20. Licensure or certification (if relevant)

_________   21. Wage comparisons to other occupations

_________   22. Total number of jobs

a. What Workers Do
b. Work Environment
c. How to Become One
d. Pay
e. Job Outlook

                                                      Chapter 1 Learn About Work

Activity 1-11 Conducting an Occupational Search

In four previous activities (1-4, 1-5, 1-6, and 1-9), you used different approaches to identify potential occupational preferences. Review these occupations and select one to use for this activity in which you will investigate a specific occupation. Go to *www.bls.gov/ooh/* and find the profile for the occupation of interest. Complete the form on this and the following page. An extra master copy of this form appears on pages 246–247.

OCCUPATIONAL SEARCH FORM

TITLE OF THE OCCUPATION ____

A. WHAT WORKERS DO

Give the definition of the occupation. _________________________________

____

____

List five major duties of the occupation.

1. ____

____

2. ____

____

3. ____

____

4. ____

____

5. ____

____

B. WORK ENVIRONMENT

Number of jobs in the occupation ______________ Year provided ______________

In what types of industries or locations do people work? _________________

____

____

Write down the normal work schedule, if provided. _______________________

____

(Continued on next page)

Chapter 1 Learn About Work

21

Activity 1-11 Conducting an Occupational Search

Describe the typical working conditions. ____

____

____

Are there unpleasant or dangerous aspects to this occupation? ____________________

____

____

C. HOW TO BECOME ONE (Education & Training, Qualification, Advancement)

What is the preferred or required level of education or training? _________________

____

List any licensure or certification requirements. ______________________________

____

List any special abilities or qualifications recommended or required. ____________

____

What opportunities are there for advancement? __________________________________

____

D. PAY

Median annual or hourly wage _____________________ Year provided _______________

Earnings: top 10% _____________________ Earnings: bottom 10% __________________

Is this occupation ABOVE or BELOW average for all occupations? __________________

E. JOB OUTLOOK

What is the expected change in employment for this occupation, 20   /   20? _______

Describe the future job prospects for this occupation. _________________________

____

____

F. SIMILAR OCCUPATIONS

List four to six occupations with similar duties. _______________________________

____

____

Which edition of the Occupational Outlook Handbook did you use for this information?
20   / 20

                                              Chapter 1 Learn About Work

Chapter 2   Career Decision Making

2-1   The Decision-making Process

Activity 2-1   **The Decision-making Process**
Objective: To use the decision-making process to make and implement a decision

2-2   Individuals and Decision Making

Activity 2-2   **Decision-making Styles**
Objective: To recognize the characteristic approach used in various styles of decision making

Activity 2-3   **Influences on Decision Making**
Objective: To describe and illustrate how various factors influence decision making

2-3   Begin Your Career

Activity 2-4   **Training Agreement Responsibilities**
Objective: To understand the responsibilities of the three parties involved in a training agreement

Activity 2-5   **Benefits of Work Experience Education**
Objective: To explain how selected individuals might benefit from work experience education

Activity 2-6   **About Work Histories**
Objective: To review what has been learned about work histories

2-4   Transferable Skills

Activity 2-7   **Transferable Skills**
Objective: To explain what is meant by each of several types of transferable skills

Activity 2-8   **Connecting Skills to Jobs**
Objective: To explain how a transferable skill might be developed into statements that could be made in a job interview

Activity 2-1   The Decision-making Process

Assume that you and several of your friends plan to go to a movie this weekend. Use the five-step decision-making process to decide which movie to go to (including the theater and time) and implement the decision. Summarize what you did at each step. Then evaluate the results. Even though choosing a movie is not a major decision, it will provide a good illustration of the process.

1. Defining the problem: ____

    ____

    ____

    ____

2. Gathering information: ____

    ____

    ____

    ____

3. Evaluating the information: ____

    ____

    ____

4. Making a choice: ____

    ____

    ____

5. Taking action: ____

    ____

    ____

6. How did the exercise turn out? Did you make a good decision? _________

    ____

    ____

                                    Chapter 2 Career Decision Making

Activity 2-2   Decision-making Styles

Assume that high school graduation is coming up shortly. What are you going to do after graduation? Explain how someone who uses the following decision-making styles would approach this decision. Then identify your decision-making style.

1. The agonizer: ____

____

____

2. The mystic: ____

____

____

3. The fatalist: ____

____

____

4. The evader: ____

____

5. The plunger: ____

____

____

6. The submissive: ____

____

____

7. The planner: ____

____

____

8. Which decision-making style do you use? ___________________________________

____

Activity 2-3   Influences on Decision Making

1. Describe a decision that you have made that was influenced by a *previous decision.*

   ____

   ____

   ____

2. Describe a decision that you have made that was influenced by *environment.*

   ____

   ____

   ____

3. Describe a decision that you have made that was influenced by *experience.*

   ____

   ____

   ____

4. Describe a decision that you have made that was influenced by *real-world restrictions.*

   ____

   ____

   ____

5. Describe a decision that you made that was influenced by *economic conditions.*

   ____

   ____

   ____

6. Give an illustration of someone (acquaintance, family member, famous person) who has overcome a reality factor to achieve a goal or to become successful.

   ____

   ____

   ____

   ____

   ____

     Chapter 2 Career Decision Making

Activity 2-4   Training Agreement Responsibilities

Work experience education involves a cooperative relationship among a student, a work experience teacher/coordinator, and an employer-supervisor. Each individual has different responsibilities. Study the training agreement used by your school or the one on page 45 of the textbook. Summarize the responsibilities of each party.

Student: ____

____

____

____

Teacher/Coordinator: ____

____

____

____

Employer-Supervisor: ____

____

____

____

Who has the primary responsibility for making this three-way partnership work? _________

____

____

Who has the authority to terminate this agreement? _________________________________

____

____

How will you be evaluated on the job? Discuss with your coordinator and supervisor and

summarize the process here. ____

____

____

____

Activity 2-5 Benefits of Work Experience Education

Explain how each of the following individuals might benefit from enrolling in a work experience education program.

1. Frank has completed one year of welding and is very good at it. But, because of the school's limited equipment, he cannot learn how to weld exotic metals such as monel, nickel, and titanium. He wants to enroll in a welding apprenticeship program after high school.

2. Amy will be a senior in the fall, but she already has enough credits to graduate. She does not want to graduate early, however, because she participates in sports and does not want to miss the exciting senior year activities. She would not mind working one-half of the day.

3. Seymour does not like any of his courses and his grades are poor. He is thinking about quitting school. What is the use in graduating, he wonders. Many of his friends are high school graduates and they cannot even get a job.

4. Carmen is an above-average student who is thinking about attending a community college after graduation. She thinks she might prepare for a technical-level health occupation but is not sure. Her high school does not have any health occupations programs.

Chapter 2 Career Decision Making

Activity 2-6   About Work Histories

Knowing about different work histories can help you think about and plan for your own career. In Chapter 2 of the textbook (pages 47–48), review the sample work histories of **Terry, Maria, Cindy**, and **Ricardo**. State several helpful facts you learned from each of the cases.

Terry: ____

____

____

Maria: ____

____

____

Cindy: ____

____

____

Ricardo: ____

____

____

Answer the following questions about the relationship between transferable skills and work histories by circling the letter T for each true statement and the letter F for each false statement.

T   F   1. Everyone has dozens of skills, and each one can be related in some way to a job.

T   F   2. To be a successful job hunter, you must be able to tell employers about what you are able to do.

T   F   3. Transferable skills can be valuable in a job search, but very few people have them.

T   F   4. Transferable skills can be used in many occupations and jobs.

T   F   5. Employers are generally only interested in job-related skills.

T   F   6. Being able to analyze facts and data is one type of transferable skill.

T   F   7. Being able to rebuild small, gasoline engines has little relationship to repairing household electrical appliances.

T   F   8. Most people have only a few occupations and jobs throughout a career.

T   F   9. Your transferable skill are often more important than your job skills.

T   F   10. Transferable skills are often developed through hobbies and volunteer work.

Activity 2-7   Transferable Skills

Explain in your own words what is meant by each of the following transferable skills.

1. Detail oriented: ____

____

____

2. Ethical behavior: ____

____

____

3. Forecasting: ____

____

4. Goal Setting: ____

____

5. Multi-lingual: ____

____

6. Nurturing: ____

____

7. Persuading: ____

____

8. Presentation abilities: ____

____

____

9. Reading body language: ____

____

____

10. Self-starter: ____

____

11. Team builder: ____

____

____

12. Time management: ____

____

____

                                    Chapter 2 Career Decision Making

Activity 2-8   Connecting Skills to Jobs

Select three of your strongest transferable skills. Follow the approach in Figure 2-6 on page 52 of the text to complete the five-step process below.

Title of job being interviewed for:	
Transferable skill:	
Declaration about transferable skill:	
Brief personal summary of how skill was obtained:	
Explain how skill will help job performance:	
Title of job being interviewed for:	
Transferable skill:	
Declaration about transferable skill:	
Brief personal summary of how skill was obtained:	
Explain how skill will help job performance:	
Title of job being interviewed for:	
Transferable skill:	
Declaration about transferable skill:	
Brief personal summary of how skill was obtained:	
Explain how skill will help job performance:	

Chapter 3   Search for a Job

3-1   Obtain a Stable Job

3-2   Job Search Preparation

3-3   Apprenticeship Programs

3-4   Job Search in the Digital Age

Activity 3-1   Different Routes to a Stable Job

Locate information in an encyclopedia or on the Web about the following recent presidents of
the United States. Summarize their work histories. Note that although their career patterns
are quite different, all the men ended up with the same job.

Bill Clinton ____

____

____

____

____

____

____

George W. Bush ____

____

____

____

____

____

____

Barack Obama ____

____

____

____

____

____

____

____

President of the United States

Activity 3-2   Controlling Your Career

Explain how the following decisions, actions, and sacrifices might pay off later.

1. Attending a local community college rather than a four-year university because that is all you can afford ____

   ____

   ____

2. Accepting a temporary or part-time job even though you would like to have a full-time, permanent position ____

   ____

   ____

3. Willingly staying after work an extra hour without pay to help finish up an important assignment ____

   ____

   ____

4. Taking pride in what you are doing and giving the job your best effort _______________

   ____

   ____

   ____

5. Taking an evening course to learn a new skill ____

   ____

   ____

6. Working evenings and weekends to earn money for college, even though you would rather be out with your friends ____

   ____

   ____

7. Reducing the number of hours worked each week to devote more time to schoolwork

   ____

   ____

   ____

Chapter 3 Search for a Job

Activity 3-3   Clarifying Job Goals

The benefits of work experience education can help you to clarify your own job goals. Which of the following benefits are most important to you? Rank them from high (1) to low (7).

Benefits	**Rank**
▪ Learn occupational skills	________
▪ Develop employability skills	________
▪ Establish a work record	________
▪ Earn while you learn	________
▪ Discover career interests and goals	________
▪ Recognize the relationship between education and work	________
▪ Remain employed after graduation	________

You will probably be asked the following question many times: "Why do you want a job?" Think about the question and write your answer.

____

____

____

____

____

____

____

____

____

____

____

____

____

____

Chapter 3 Search for a Job

Activity 3-4   Applying for a Social Security Number

Prepare to apply for a Social Security number by filling out the sample application that follows. Encourage students to accurately record all information and to note the required evidence of age, citizenship, and identity.

SOCIAL SECURITY ADMINISTRATION
Application for a Social Security Card

Form Approved
OMB No. 0960-0066

1

NAME TO BE SHOWN ON CARD	First	Full Middle Name	Last
FULL NAME AT BIRTH IF OTHER THAN ABOVE	First	Full Middle Name	Last
OTHER NAMES USED			

2 Social Security number previously assigned to the person listed in item 1 ☐☐☐ - ☐☐ - ☐☐☐☐

3 PLACE OF BIRTH ________________________ (Do Not Abbreviate)   City   State or Foreign Country   Office Use Only   FCI

4 DATE OF BIRTH ____________ MM/DD/YYYY

5 CITIZENSHIP (Check One)
☐ U.S. Citizen   ☐ Legal Alien Allowed To Work   ☐ Legal Alien Not Allowed To Work(See Instructions On Page 3)   ☐ Other (See Instructions On Page 3)

6 ETHNICITY
Are You Hispanic or Latino? (Your Response is Voluntary)   ☐ Yes   ☐ No

7 RACE
Select One or More (Your Response is Voluntary)
☐ Native Hawaiian   ☐ American Indian   ☐ Other Pacific Islander
☐ Alaska Native   ☐ Black/African American   ☐ White
☐ Asian

8 SEX   ☐ Male   ☐ Female

9

A. PARENT/ MOTHER'S NAME AT HER BIRTH	First	Full Middle Name	Last

B. PARENT/ MOTHER'S SOCIAL SECURITY NUMBER (See instructions for 9 B on Page 3)   ☐☐☐ - ☐☐ - ☐☐☐☐   ☐ Unknown

10

A. PARENT/ FATHER'S NAME	First	Full Middle Name	Last

B. PARENT/ FATHER'S SOCIAL SECURITY NUMBER (See instructions for 10B on Page 3)   ☐☐☐ - ☐☐ - ☐☐☐☐   ☐ Unknown

11 Has the person listed in item 1 or anyone acting on his/her behalf ever filed for or received a Social Security number card before?
☐ Yes (If "yes" answer questions 12-13)   ☐ No   ☐ Don't Know (If "don't know," skip to question 14.)

12

Name shown on the most recent Social Security card issued for the person listed in item 1	First	Full Middle Name	Last

13 Enter any different date of birth if used on an earlier application for a card ________________ MM/DD/YYYY

14 TODAY'S DATE ____________ MM/DD/YYYY

15 DAYTIME PHONE NUMBER ________ Area Code ________ Number

16 MAILING ADDRESS (Do Not Abbreviate)   Street Address, Apt. No., PO Box, Rural Route No.   City   State/Foreign Country   ZIP Code

I declare under penalty of perjury that I have examined all the information on this form, and on any accompanying statements or forms, and it is true and correct to the best to my knowledge.

17 YOUR SIGNATURE

18 YOUR RELATIONSHIP TO THE PERSON IN ITEM 1 IS:
☐ Self   ☐ Natural Or Adoptive Parent   ☐ Legal Guardian   ☐ Other   Specify ________

DO NOT WRITE BELOW THIS LINE (FOR SSA USE ONLY)

NPN			DOC	NTI	CAN		ITV
PBC	EVI	EVA	EVC	PRA	NWR	DNR	UNIT

EVIDENCE SUBMITTED	SIGNATURE AND TITLE OF EMPLOYEE(S) REVIEWING EVIDENCE AND/OR CONDUCTING INTERVIEW
	DATE
	DCL DATE

Form SS-5 (08-2011) ef (08-2011)   Destroy Prior Editions   Page 5

Activity 3-5   Apprenticeship

Complete the following word puzzle by filling in the correct terms.

```
 1 |   |   |   | A |   |   |   |   |
 2 |   |   |   | P |   |   |   |   |   |   |
 3 |   |   |   | P |   |   |   |   |   |
 4 |   |   |   | R |   |   |   |   |
 5 |   |   |   | E |   |   |   |   |   |
 6 |   |   |   | N |   |   |   |   |
 7 |   |   |   | T |   |   |   |
 8 |   |   |   | I |   |   |   |
 9 |   |   |   | C |   |   |
10 |   |   |   | E |   |   |   |
11 |   |   |   | S |   |   |   |
12 |   |   |   | H |   |   |   |
13 |   |   |   | I |   |
14 |   |   |   | P |   |   |   |
```

Across

1. The proportion of pay generally earned by an apprentice compared to that of an experienced worker

2. A worker who is enrolled in an apprenticeship program

3. An apprentice who works for an employer

4. Upon completion of an apprenticeship program, the person becomes a journey _______________

5, The knowledge, skill, and know-how that is gained during participation in an apprenticeship program

6. Certain government requirements that registered apprenticeship programs must meet

7. An important type of training received by many apprentices

8. A characteristic of apprenticeship programs that makes entry difficult

9. One who completes the required forms and tests for entrance into an apprenticeship program

10. Having a position as part of a union

11. Organizations that support and manage apprenticeship programs

12. A type of skill learned in many apprenticeship program

13. An apprenticeship waiting list

14. The name given to a group of similar tasks that a person performs for pay

Chapter 3 Search for a Job

Activity 3-6   Apprenticeship Interview

A person applying for entry into an apprenticeship program is required to complete an interview. A sample form used by interviewers to rate an applicant appears below. Fill out the form in relation to your view of yourself. Be honest in your ratings.

PART III. SUMMARY OF FACTORS (to be filled out by the Committee member during the interview.)

Education: Survey of high school and college courses beyond those directly applicable to the trade

Poor background. Took minimum academic courses. Poor grades.	
Fair background. Some academic electives. Grades below average.	
Medium background. Average course electives with fair grades.	
Good background. College-prep or some college work.	
Excellent background. Extra subjects, college or post-high school with good grades.	

Remarks: ____

Physical Factors: Physical ability to perform requirements of the classification, lost time, health history, stamina, family health

Unsatisfactory because:	
Doubtful—verification needed:	
Satisfactory	

Interest: Desire to be a craftsperson, reasons for choosing this trade, knowledge of the trade, etc., interest in relevant hobbies

Total lack of interest (just wants a job)		Displays a real interest	
Little interest. Past associations show very slight interest.		Manifests a strong desire to be a craftsman	
Fair interest indicated by past associations and hobbies			

Remarks: ____

Attitude: Physical Has he or she ever done any hard work? How was school attendance? Will he or she work under supervision? Has applicant participated in any organized groups, extracurricular activities, or sports? Examine past employment, school activities, and military records.

Unacceptable	Poor	Fair	Good	Excellent

Remarks: ____

Personal Traits: Appearance, assertiveness, sincerity, dependability, character, and habits

Unacceptable	Poor	Fair	Good	Excellent

Remarks: ____

After careful consideration of all factors, my grade for this applicant is (write an exact numerical grade such as 67, 83, or 95)

0   10   20   30   40   50   60   70   80   90   100

(Interviewer)   (Date)

Chapter 3 Search for a Job

Activity 3-7   Reading Help-Wanted Ads

Abbreviations are often used in help-wanted ads to save space. The following are a number of abbreviations found in newspaper classified ads. Write out the meaning of each.

appt _______________________________   info _______________________________

ASAP _______________________________   lic'd _______________________________

ass't _______________________________   lve _______________________________

avail _______________________________   M/F/D/V _______________________________

cert _______________________________   mfg _______________________________

deg _______________________________   mgr _______________________________

DFWR _______________________________   MS Off _______________________________

EDP _______________________________   OT _______________________________

EOE _______________________________   OTR driver _______________________________

eves & wknds _______________________________   ref _______________________________

exp pref'd _______________________________   req'd _______________________________

flex hrs _______________________________   sales rep _______________________________

fringes _______________________________   sal neg _______________________________

f/time _______________________________   temp _______________________________

hrly _______________________________   trng _______________________________

hvy equip _______________________________   WPM _______________________________

Look at the help-wanted ads in a newspaper and see if you can identify additional abbreviations not listed. Write the abbreviations and their meaning on the lines that follow.

_______________________   _______________________

_______________________   _______________________

_______________________   _______________________

_______________________   _______________________

_______________________   _______________________

_______________________   _______________________

_______________________   _______________________

Chapter 3 Search for a Job

Activity 3-8 Sources of Job Leads

The most common sources of job leads are listed. Consult each source and try to write down at least one lead. Check off (✓) each source after you have made the contact(s).

______ Relatives

______ Neighbors

______ Friends

______ Work experience coordinator

______ Guidance counselor

______ School placement officer

______ Help-wanted ads

______ CareerOneStop

______ Private employment agency

______ Employer contact

______ Telephone Yellow Pages (or YP.com)

______ Web-based job banks and portals

______ Social networks

Activity 3-9   Following Through

For each of these situations, write down what the person could do to follow through and try to get a job.

1. Alberto learns from his guidance counselor about a good position. It is the last day to apply. He gets himself ready and drives to the business. The receptionist is not very helpful. She tells Alberto that she is a temporary employee and is not sure whom to call. She is quite busy.

____

____

____

2. On Saturday, Sarah learns that her friend's mother is looking for immediate help in her day-care center and has placed an ad in the Sunday paper. It is exactly the kind of job that Sarah wants.

____

____

____

3. David is passing by a sandwich shop when he sees a help-wanted sign in the front window. When he walks in, he finds that there are six people ahead of him, all applying for the same job. David wonders whether it is worth applying or whether he should come back later

____

____

4. Late one afternoon, Mei-ling sees a posting at her school placement office for an assistant at a pet store. She knows the pet store and would like to work there. It is the last day for receiving applications. The ad says to apply in writing.

____

____

5. Tina's sister is leaving her job at a clothing shop at the mall to return to college. She mentions to Tina that a lot of jobs will be opening up at the mall with college students going back to school.

____

____

____

Chapter 4   Apply for a Job

4-1   Data Sheets and Job Applications

Activity 4-1   **Job Application Documents and Methods**
Objective: To review characteristics of documents and methods used to apply for a job

Activity 4-2   **Personal Data Sheet**
Objective: To prepare a personal data sheet

Activity 4-3   **Job Application Form (Private Employer)**
Objective: To practice filling out a job application form

Activity 4-4   **Job Application Form (Government Employer)**
Objective: To practice filling out a job application form

4-2   Write a Resume

Activity 4-5   **Resume**
Objective: To prepare a job resume

4-3   Contact Employers

Activity 4-6   **Letter of Application**
Objective: To write a sample letter of application

Activity 4-7   **Pre-employment Tests**
Objective: To become familiar with the nature of a general ability test

Activity 4-1   Job Application Documents

Test your knowledge of the types of documents and methods used to apply for a job by completing the following two exercises.

Part 1: Match the document (a, b, or c) with the statement below that best describes it.

a. Personal data sheet
b. Job application form
c. Resume

_______ 1. Helps employers screen applicants for interviews.

_______ 2. Contains a short statement of career goals.

_______ 3. Contains complete, detailed information, even though some data may not always be used.

_______ 4. Sent with a cover letter when applying for a job by mail.

_______ 5. Should be checked carefully before mailing or giving to an employer.

_______ 6. Never given directly to an employer.

_______ 7. Provides job seekers with information normally required by employers.

_______ 8. Usually limited to one page.

_______ 9. First of the three types of documents to be completed.

_______ 10. May be brief or quite detailed.

Part 2: Match the job application method (a, b, c, or d) with the statement below that best describes it.

a. Applying in person
b. Applying by telephone
c. Applying in writing (letter of application)
d. Applying online

_______ 11. A job seeker can make more contacts in less time this way.

_______ 12. This is similar to going for a job interview.

_______ 13. Its purpose is to attract and hold an employer's interest.

_______ 14. It is important to be organized before contacting an employer this way.

_______ 15. Good verbal skills are important with this method.

_______ 16. This method also calls attention to the resume.

_______ 17. For this method, you may use keywords relating to the position you want.

_______ 18. First impressions are important with this method.

_______ 19. This kind of application may be made in several ways.

_______ 20. This may result in the immediate need to complete a job application form.

Chapter 4 Apply for a Job

Activity 4-2   Personal Data Sheet

A personal data sheet is useful in completing job application forms and in developing a resume. Complete the following form by filling in each item that applies to you.

PERSONAL DATA SHEET

IDENTIFICATION

Name ____ Soc. Sec. # ________________

Address ____

Telephone (____) ____

E-mail Address ____

Hobbies/Interests ____

Honors/Awards/Offices

____

Sports/Activities ____

Other ____

EDUCATIONAL BACKGROUND

	Dates Attended	
School Name and Address	From:	To:
High School:		
Course of Study ____________ Rank ____________		GPA ________
Favorite Subject(s) ____________		
Other (College, Trade, Business, or Correspondence School):	From:	To:
Course of Study ____________ Rank ____________		GPA ________
Favorite Subject(s) ____________		
Other (College, Trade, Business, or Correspondence School):	From:	To:
Course of Study ____________ Rank ____________		GPA ________

(Continued on next page)

                                                    Chapter 4 Apply for a Job

Activity 4-2   Personal Data Sheet

EMPLOYMENT HISTORY

(Start with present or most recent employer.)

1. Company ___________________________________ Telephone ( ) ___________________
Address ____
Employed from Mo. ______ Yr. ______ /to Mo. ______ Yr. ______ Supervisor _____________
Position/Title ____
Last Wage ___________ Reason for Leaving ____

2. Company ___________________________________ Telephone ( ) ___________________
Address ____
Employed from Mo. ______ Yr. ______ /to Mo. ______ Yr. ______ Supervisor _____________
Position/Title ____
Last Wage ___________ Reason for Leaving ____

3. Company ___________________________________ Telephone ( ) ___________________
Address ____
Employed from Mo. ______ Yr. ______ /to Mo. ______ Yr. ______ Supervisor _____________
Position/Title ____
Last Wage ___________ Reason for Leaving ____

REFERENCES

1. Name _______________________________ Title ___________________________________
Address ____
Relationship _______________________________ Telephone ( ) ___________________

2. Name _______________________________ Title ___________________________________
Address ____
Relationship _______________________________ Telephone ( ) ___________________

3. Name _______________________________ Title ___________________________________
Address ____
Relationship _______________________________ Telephone ( ) ___________________

Activity 4-3   Job Application Form (Private Employer)

Prepare to complete a job application form by filling out the following sample. Use the personal data sheet you completed in the previous activity.

EMPLOYMENT APPLICATION

This company is an equal opportunity employer and does not discriminate in hiring or in terms or conditions of employment because of race, color, creed, religion, national origin, sex, age, or disability. This company only hires individuals authorized for employment in the United States.

Position applying for: _______________________________________ Today's date: _______________

Schedule desired: (   ) Full-time   (   ) Temporary   (   ) Part-time   Salary required: _______________

PERSONAL INFORMATION

Name: ____

Address: ____
              Street   City   State   ZIP

How long have you lived there (years/months)? _______ / _______   Phone: ____________________
                                                                          Years   Months

Previous address: ____
                          Street   City   State   ZIP

How long did you live there (years/months)? _______ / _______   Phone: ____________________
                                                              Years   Months

Age (if under 18): _________ Social Security number: ___________________________________

Are you authorized for employment in the United States? (   ) Yes   (   ) No

EDUCATION

High school: ____
                    Name   City   State

Degree/area of study: ______________________ Years attended: ____________ Graduated? (   ) Yes (   ) No

College: ____
                  Name   City   State

Degree/area of study: ______________________ Years attended: ____________ Graduated? (   ) Yes (   ) No

Graduate school: ____
                            Name   City   State

Degree/area of study: ______________________ Years attended: ____________ Graduated? (   ) Yes (   ) No

Other: ____
                Name   City   State

Degree/area of study: ______________________ Years attended: ____________ Graduated? (   ) Yes (   ) No

SKILLS

Describe skills relevant to the position applied for: _____________________________________

____

Chapter 4 Apply for a Job

Activity 4-3   Job Application Form
(Private Employer)

EMPLOYMENT HISTORY

List employment starting with your most recent position. Continue on a separate page as needed. Account for any time during this period that you were unemployed on a separate page. If you have fewer than three places of employment, please provide three personal references on a separate page.

May we contact your present employer?   (   ) Yes   (   ) No

Employer: ____
                    Name   Street

City _________________ State _______________ ZIP _________ Phone _________ E-mail _________

Job title: _______________________ Responsibilities: ____

Start date: _________ End date: _________ Supervisor: _______________________________________

Starting wage: _______ Final wage: _______ Reason for leaving: _______________________________

Employer: ____
                    Name   Street

City _________________ State _______________ ZIP _________ Phone _________ E-mail _________

Job title: _______________________ Responsibilities: ____

Start date: _________ End date: _________ Supervisor: _______________________________________

Starting wage: _________ Final wage: _________ Reason for leaving: ___________________________

Employer: ____
                    Name   Street

City _________________ State _______________ ZIP _________ Phone _________ E-mail _________

Job title: _______________________ Responsibilities: ____

Start date: _________ End date: _________ Supervisor: _______________________________________

Starting wage: _________ Final wage: _________ Reason for leaving: ___________________________

MISCELLANEOUS

Have you been employed by this company before?   (   ) Yes   (   ) No   If you answered yes, please indicate dates and positions: ____

List relatives or acquaintances employed by this company: _______________________________________

Have you ever been convicted of a crime?   (   ) Yes   (   ) No   If you answered yes, please explain: _________

I hereby affirm that the information I have given on this application is complete and accurate. I understand that any falsification or omission will be grounds for immediate dismissal. I authorize a thorough investigation in connection with this application and authorize the release of documents and personal interviews with third parties, such as prior employers, family members, and business associates. If hired, I agree that my employment and compensation can be terminated without cause or notice at any time at the option of the company or myself. I understand that no representative of the company, other than a Vice President, has the authority to enter into any agreement for employment for any specified period of time or to make any agreement contrary to the foregoing.

Signature_________________________________   Date_________________________________

Chapter 4 Apply for a Job

Activity 4-4   Job Application Form
(Government Employer)

This is a typical form used in hiring various civil service classifications. Complete the form by filling in each item that applies to you.

APPLICATION FOR CIVIL SERVICE EMPLOYMENT

Last Name _________________________ First Name _________________________ Middle Name _________

Address ____

City _________________________________ State _________ ZIP _________ County _____________

Home Phone _________________________ Work Phone _________________________

Social Security Number _________________________________ Age (if under 18) _____________________

If applying for a **vacant position,** fill in the information below:

Job title _________________________ Position Control No. (PCN) ____________ Deadline ________

If applying for a **civil service examination,** fill in the information below.

Exam Title _________________________ Exam No. _________________________ Deadline ________

Type of work desired: ____ ☐ Full-time   ☐ Part-Time

1   Do you claim veterans' preference?   ☐ Yes   ☐ No

2.   Have you ever been a state or county employee?   ☐ Yes   ☐ No

      If you are currently a state employee: Job Title _________________________ Job No. ________

3.   Have you ever been convicted of a felony?   ☐ Yes   ☐ No

      A felony conviction will not necessarily be a bar to employment.

4.   Have you ever been suspended or discharged from any position?   ☐ Yes   ☐ No

If you answered yes to Question 2, 3, or 4, please explain fully _________________________________

____

LICENSES, REGISTRATIONS, AND CERTIFICATES

Be sure to include any valid driver's license or commercial drivers license if required for the job.

Issued by	Field/Trade/Specialization	License/Certificate No.	Expires

EDUCATION

Circle highest grade completed   1   2   3   4   5   6   7   8   9   10   11   12   GED

Circle full academic year of college completed   1   2   3   4   5   6   7   8

School Name and Location	Major Area(s) of Study	Degree or Certification

Are you currently attending school (or intern positions)?   ☐ Yes   ☐ No   Level _________________

List schools attended after high school. Include technical, business, and professional schools and colleges.

48

Activity 4-4 Job Application Form (Government Employer)

List any relevant course work you have taken at the high school level or beyond relevant to the position or examination for which you are applying.

TRAINING AND OTHER QUALIFICATIONS

Subject or Title	Organization	Length of Training

List special equipment or machines you can operate. ____

List computer software in which you have skill, including word processing, spreadsheet, and database programs. Please indicate the name of the specific software. ____

List special clerical skills, including keying and shorthand. ____
____ Keying speed:___________

List any additional relevant skills you have. ____

List your past work experience beginning with your most recent employment. Use additional sheets if necessary.

Name, address, and phone number of employing firm ____
____ Dates ___________________

Supervisor _______________ Job title _______________ Reason for leaving ___________

Salary _________ Description of work ____

Name, address, and phone number of employing firm ____
____ Dates ___________________

Supervisor _______________ Job title _______________ Reason for leaving ___________

Salary _________ Description of work ____

Name, address, and phone number of employing firm ____
____ Dates ___________________

Supervisor _______________ Job title _______________ Reason for leaving ___________

Salary _________ Description of work ____

Name, address, and phone number of employing firm ____
____ Dates ___________________

Supervisor _______________ Job title _______________ Reason for leaving ___________

Salary _________ Description of work ____

I certify that the information I have supplied in this application is true and complete to the best of my knowledge. I understand that if this application is not completed in full, it will not be processed and I will be disqualified. I understand that a background check may be required prior to employment and that drug testing may be required. I consent that my past employers may disclose any information relevant to my employment to the agency to which I am applying. I understand that any offer of employment is contingent upon proof of legal authorization to work in the United States as required by the Immigration Reform and Control Act.

Signature ____ Date _______________________

Chapter 4 Apply for a Job

49

Activity 4-5   Resume

Prepare a draft of a resume by following the outline below. Refer to your personal data sheet as necessary. After your instructor has reviewed your draft, key your resume, proofread it, and make any corrections that are needed. Then have your resume duplicated for distribution to potential employers. Do not exceed one page.

OBJECTIVE: ____

____

____

EXPERIENCE: ____

____

____

____

EDUCATION: ____

____

____

____

REFERENCES:

_____________________________   _____________________________

_____________________________   _____________________________

_____________________________   _____________________________

_____________________________   _____________________________

Chapter 4 Apply for a Job

Activity 4-6   Letter of Application

Write a draft of a letter applying for a real or hypothetical job. Follow the four guidelines on pages 102 and 103 of your text. After the letter has been reviewed by your instructor, format it correctly, key it neatly, and proofread it as discussed on page 104 and illustrated on page 103.

____

____

____

____

____

Dear _________________________________

____

____

____

____

____

____

____

____

____

____

____

____

Sincerely

____

Enclosure

Chapter 4 Apply for a Job

Activity 4-7   Pre-employment Tests

One type of pre-employment test is a general ability test. This type of test measures basic academic knowledge and skills. Answer the following questions and you will have an idea of what such tests are like.

General Science

1. An eclipse of the sun throws the shadow of the

   a. moon on the sun.
   b. moon on the earth.
   c. earth on the sun.
   d. earth on the moon.

2. Substances that hasten chemical reaction time without themselves undergoing change are called

   a. buffers.
   b. colloids.
   c. reducers.
   d. catalysts.

Word Knowledge

3. If the wind is *variable* today, that means it is

   a. mild.
   b. steady.
   c. shifting.
   d. chilling

4. *Rudiments* most nearly means

   a. politics.
   b. minute details.
   c. promotion opportunities.
   d. basic methods and procedures.

Understanding Paragraphs

5. Twenty-five percent of all household burglaries can be attributed to unlocked windows or doors. Crime is the result of opportunity plus desire. To prevent crime, each individual has the responsibility to

   a. provide the desire.
   b. provide the opportunity.
   c. prevent the desire.
   d. prevent the opportunity.

Math Knowledge

6. If x + 6 = 7, what does × equal?

   a. 0
   b. 1
   c. −1
   d. 7/8

7. What is the area of this square?

   a. 1 square foot
   b. 5 square feet
   c. 10 square feet
   d. 25 square feet

Chapter 4 Apply for a Job

Activity 4-7   Pre-employment Tests

Math Reasoning

8. How many 35-passenger buses would it take to carry 144 people?

   a. 3
   b. 4
   c. 5
   d. 6

9. It costs $0.50 per square yard to waterproof canvas. What will it cost to waterproof a canvas truck cover that is 15′ × 24′?

   a. $6.67
   b. $18.00
   c. $20.00
   d. $180.00

Mechanical Knowledge

10. Which post holds up the greater part of the load?

   a. Post A
   b. Post B
   c. both equal
   d. not clear

11. In this arrangement of pulleys, which pulley turns the fastest?

   a. A
   b. B
   c. C
   d. D

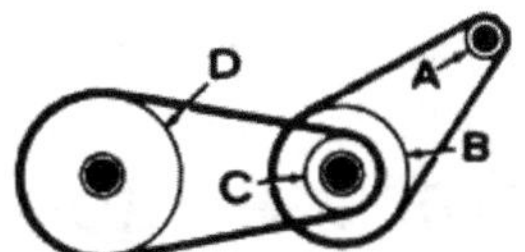

Electronics Information

12. Which of the following has the least resistance?

   a. wood
   b. iron
   c. rubber
   d. silver

13. In this circuit diagram, the resistance is 100 ohms and the current is 0.1 amperes. The voltage is

   a. 5 volts.
   b. 10 volts.
   c. 100 volts
   d. 1,000 volts

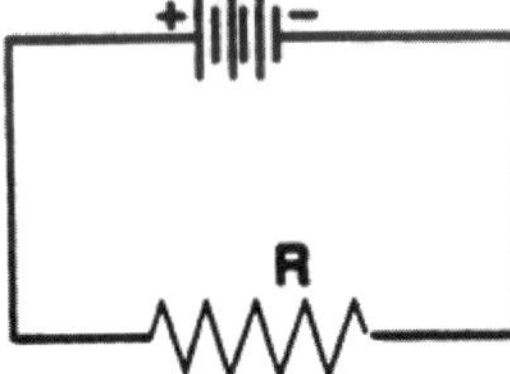

Auto and Shop Information

14. A car uses too much oil when which part is worn?

   a. pistons
   b. piston rings
   c. main bearings
   d. connecting rods

15. The saw shown below is used mainly to cut

   a. plywood
   b. odd-shaped holes in wood.
   c. along the grain of the wood.
   d. across the grain of the wood.

Reproduced from *ASVAB 18/19 Counselor Manual,* July 1992

Chapter 5   Interview for a Job

5-1   Before the Interview

Activity 5-1   **Interviewer's Questions, I**
Objective: To prepare responses to standard questions asked at a job interview

Activity 5-2   **Interviewer's Questions, II**
Objective: prepare responses to potential interview questions related to a specific company and job

Activity 5-3   **Background Research**
Objective: To learn about the work performed in various types of companies

5-2   During the Interview

Activity 5-4   **Preparing for a Job Interview**
Objective: To develop sample questions and comments in preparation for a job interview

5-3   After the Interview

Activity 5-5   **Follow-up Letter**
Objective: To practice writing a follow-up letter

Activity 5-1   Interviewer's Questions, I

Even though an interviewer will probably look over your job application form and resume in advance, he or she may still ask a number of basic questions. Be prepared by thinking about and writing an answer to the following questions:

1. Tell me something about yourself. ____

____

____

2. What type of work do your parents or family do? ____________________________

____

____

3. What are your best and worst subjects in school? ____________________________

____

____

4. What do you like to do in your spare time? _________________________________

____

____

5. If I called one of the persons you listed as a reference, what do you think he or she would

   say about you? ____

____

____

6. What types of previous jobs have you held? _________________________________

____

____

7. Were you ever fired from a previous job? If so, why? ________________________

____

____

8. What do you want to be doing five years from now? __________________________

____

____

Activity 5-2   Interviewer's Questions, II

In addition to basic questions such as those in the previous activity, an interviewer may ask more specific questions about you and the job you are interested in. Name a company and a job you are applying for and then answer the following questions in relation to them.

Company _______________________________   Job Title _______________________________

1. Why did you apply for a job with us? _______________________________

____

____

2. What do you know about the type of work we do here? _______________________________

____

____

3. Why do you think you would like this type of work? _______________________________

____

____

4. What specific job skills do you have? _______________________________

____

____

5. If I hired you, how long would you expect to stay with us? _______________________________

____

____

6. How much would you expect to be paid? _______________________________

____

____

7. I have a number of qualified applicants for this job. Why should I hire you? _______________________________

____

____

8. What questions would you like to ask me? _______________________________

____

Chapter 5 Interview for a Job

Activity 5-3   Background Research

Before going to a job interview, you should learn something about the type of industry in which the job is located. Use the *North American Industry Classification System* to search for information. Go to *www.census.gov/naics/2007/NAICOD07.HTM*, and key the name of the occupational establishment in the search window. You could also use an encyclopedia or an Internet search engine.

1. Alumina refining: ____

____

2. Boiler casings manufacturing: ____

____

3. Commodity contracts trader: ____

____

4. Floriculture production (formerly ornamental floriculturist): ____________________

____

5. Freight forwarding company: ____

____

6. Holding companies: ____

____

7. Limestone mining or quarrying: ____

____

8. Lithographic printing: ____

____

9. News service syndicate: ____

____

10. Outpatient care center: ____

____

11. Operative builders: ____

____

12. Timber tract operations (formerly lumber jobber) ______________________________

____

Chapter 5 Interview for a Job

Activity 5-4   Preparing for a Job Interview

A job interview involves two-way communications. Identify a job that you would like to have. List five questions that you might want to ask the interviewer.

Job: ____

____

1. ____

____

2. ____

____

3. ____

____

4. ____

____

5. ____

____

Many job applicants fail to ask for the job. Before you leave the interview, tell the interviewer if you want the job. Provide an example here of what you might say:

____

____

____

____

Assume that the interviewer offers you the job. List below any questions you might ask or statements you might make before accepting or rejecting the job.

____

____

____

____

Chapter 5 Interview for a Job

Activity 5-5   Follow-up Letter

Assume that you have had an interview with Ms. Karen Judkins, Personnel Manager of the Ozark State Bank, for a job as a teller. She will not make a decision for about a week, until several other applicants have been interviewed. You would like to have the job. Write a draft of an appropriate follow-up letter. Follow the guidelines on pages 126 and 127 of the text. The bank's address is 14 Main St., Leslie, AR 72465-1105.

____

____

____

____

____

____

____

Dear ____

____

____

____

____

____

____

____

____

____

Sincerely

____

Chapter 5 Interview for a Job

Chapter 6   Begin a New Job

Activity 6-1   Employee Orientation Program

1. A packet of information is mailed to you prior to the orientation meeting. ______________

   ____

   ____

   ____

2. When you arrive at the orientation site, a friendly company representative greets you

   and directs you where to sit. ____

   ____

3. A company representative introduces a 15-minute video about the company. ___________

   ____

   ____

   ____

4. The human resources director explains the nature and purpose of the HR Department.

   ____

   ____

   ____

5. A folder containing various forms and information sheets is passed out which you will

   then complete. ____

   ____

   ____

6 An Employee Handbook is given each new employee. You are asked to read it during the

   next week and return a signed form, which indicates that you have read and understand

   the contents. ____

   ____

   ____

7. Following the formal meeting, you are directed to the company cafeteria for a compli-

   mentary buffet, after which you report to your designated department. ______________

   ____

   ____

   ____

Activity 6-2 Organizational Structure

Diagram the organizational structure for the company in which you are employed. If you do not have a job, use your school system.

Draw an arrow to indicate your position in the organization. Describe the chain of command that you would follow if you wanted to pursue a complaint to the highest level of authority in the organization. Also, draw this path in your figure using a colored marking pen or highlighter.

____

____

____

____

____

____

____

Activity 6-3   Policies and Rules

The following are a number of typical statements found in a company policy manual or employee handbook. Assume that you are the employer. Explain the reason for each policy or rule.

1. Each employee must punch his or her own time card when beginning or ending work.

   ____

   ____

2. An employee is docked 15 minutes' pay for each quarter-hour period in which he or she is late. (For example, a person who clocks in at 7:03 is figured for payroll purposes as having started work at 7:15.)

   ____

   ____

3. If you are ill or cannot come to work, notify your immediate supervisor as early as possible, but no later than the scheduled starting time for your shift.

   ____

   ____

4. Company supplies, tools, or equipment may not be removed from company premises. Employees found in violation of this rule face disciplinary action or possible termination.

   ____

   ____

5. Local personal phone calls during working hours should be kept to a minimum. Long-distance personal calls charged to the company are prohibited.

   ____

   ____

6. Each employee who has completed the probationary period is eligible for two weeks (ten days) of paid vacation. The vacation period must be requested through and approved by your immediate supervisor.

   ____

   ____

7. Two-week written notification is required for voluntarily terminating employment. Submit a letter to your immediate supervisor.

   ____

   ____

Activity 6-4   Completing a Form W-4

One of the first things you will do after being hired is to complete a Form W-4. The information you provide on the form will be used by the employer to withhold the correct amount of federal income tax from your paycheck. Learn how to complete the form by filling out the Personal Allowances Worksheet and practice Form W-4 below. Your instructor will provide additional information regarding line E and any other worksheets that might apply.

Personal Allowances Worksheet (Keep for your records.)

A   Enter "1" for **yourself** if no one else can claim you as a dependent . . . . **A** ______

B   Enter "1" if: {
 • You are single and have only one job; or
 • You are married, have only one job, and your spouse does not work; or
 • Your wages from a second job or your spouse's wages (or the total of both) are $1,500 or less.
} . . . **B** ______

C   Enter "1" for your **spouse.** But, you may choose to enter "-0-" if you are married and have either a working spouse or more than one job. (Entering "-0-" may help you avoid having too little tax withheld.) . . . . **C** ______

D   Enter number of **dependents** (other than your spouse or yourself) you will claim on your tax return . . . . **D** ______

E   Enter "1" if you will file as **head of household** on your tax return (see conditions under **Head of household** above) . . **E** ______

F   Enter "1" if you have at least $1,900 of **child or dependent care expenses** for which you plan to claim a credit . . . **F** ______
     (**Note.** Do **not** include child support payments. See Pub. 503, Child and Dependent Care Expenses, for details.)

G   **Child Tax Credit** (including additional child tax credit). See Pub. 972, Child Tax Credit, for more information.
     • If your total income will be less than $61,000 ($90,000 if married), enter "2" for each eligible child; then **less** "1" if you have three to seven eligible children or **less** "2" if you have eight or more eligible children.
     • If your total income will be between $61,000 and $84,000 ($90,000 and $119,000 if married), enter "1" for each eligible child . . . **G** ______

H   Add lines A through G and enter total here. (**Note.** This may be different from the number of exemptions you claim on your tax return.) ▶ **H** ______

For accuracy, complete all worksheets that apply. {
 • If you plan to **itemize** or **claim adjustments to income** and want to reduce your withholding, see the **Deductions and Adjustments Worksheet** on page 2.
 • If you are **single** and have more than one job or are **married and you and your spouse both work** and the combined earnings from all jobs exceed $40,000 ($10,000 if married), see the **Two-Earners/Multiple Jobs Worksheet** on page 2 to avoid having too little tax withheld.
 • If **neither** of the above situations applies, **stop here** and enter the number from line H on line 5 of Form W-4 below.
}

-------------------------- **Separate here and give Form W-4 to your employer. Keep the top part for your records.** --------------------------

Form **W-4**			
Department of the Treasury Internal Revenue Service	**Employee's Withholding Allowance Certificate** ▶ Whether you are entitled to claim a certain number of allowances or exemption from withholding is subject to review by the IRS. Your employer may be required to send a copy of this form to the IRS.	OMB No. 1545-0074	20**12**

1 Your first name and middle initial	Last name	**2** Your social security number
Home address (number and street or rural route)	**3** ☐ Single ☐ Married ☐ Married, but withhold at higher Single rate. Note. If married, but legally separated, or spouse is a nonresident alien, check the "Single" box.	
City or town, state, and ZIP code	**4** If your last name differs from that shown on your social security card, check here. You must call 1-800-772-1213 for a replacement card. ▶ ☐	

5   Total number of allowances you are claiming (from line **H** above **or** from the applicable worksheet on page 2) . . . **5** ______

6   Additional amount, if any, you want withheld from each paycheck . . . . **6** $ ______

7   I claim exemption from withholding for 2012, and I certify that I meet **both** of the following conditions for exemption.
     • Last year I had a right to a refund of **all** federal income tax withheld because I had **no** tax liability, **and**
     • This year I expect a refund of **all** federal income tax withheld because I expect to have **no** tax liability.
     If you meet both conditions, write "Exempt" here . . . . ▶ | **7** |

Under penalties of perjury, I declare that I have examined this certificate and, to the best of my knowledge and belief, it is true, correct, and complete.

Employee's signature
(This form is not valid unless you sign it.) ▶ _______________________   **Date** ▶ _______________

8 Employer's name and address (Employer: Complete lines 8 and 10 only if sending to the IRS.)	**9** Office code (optional)	**10** Employer identification number (EIN)

For Privacy Act and Paperwork Reduction Act Notice, see page 2.   Cat. No. 10220Q   Form **W-4** (2012)

   Chapter 6 Begin a New Job

Activity 6-5   Payroll Withholding

The following is part of the table an employer uses to figure the amount of income tax to be withheld from the weekly paycheck of a single person. Use the chart as required to answer the questions that follow.

SINGLE Persons—WEEKLY Payroll Period
(For Wages Paid through December 2012)

And the wages are—		And the number of withholding allowances claimed is—										
At least	But less than	0	1	2	3	4	5	6	7	8	9	10
		The amount of income tax to be withheld is—										
195	200	16	8	1	0	0	0	0	0	0	0	0
200	210	16	9	2	0	0	0	0	0	0	0	0
210	220	18	10	3	0	0	0	0	0	0	0	0
220	230	19	11	4	0	0	0	0	0	0	0	0
230	240	21	12	5	0	0	0	0	0	0	0	0
240	250	22	13	6	0	0	0	0	0	0	0	0
250	260	24	14	7	0	0	0	0	0	0	0	0
260	270	25	15	8	0	0	0	0	0	0	0	0
270	280	27	16	9	1	0	0	0	0	0	0	0
280	290	28	17	10	2	0	0	0	0	0	0	0
290	300	30	19	11	3	0	0	0	0	0	0	0
300	310	31	20	12	4	0	0	0	0	0	0	0
310	320	33	22	13	5	0	0	0	0	0	0	0
320	330	34	23	14	6	0	0	0	0	0	0	0
330	349	36	25	15	7	0	0	0	0	0	0	0
340	350	37	26	16	8	1	0	0	0	0	0	0

1. How much income tax should be withheld for the following individuals?

   $225 in wages, 1 allowance claimed ______________________________

   $270 in wages, 3 allowances ______________________________

   $315 in wages, 0 allowances claimed ______________________________

2. Why might a single person claim more than 1 allowance?

   ____

3. Why might an individual not claim any allowances (put down 0) even though he or she is entitled to allowances?

   ____

   ____

4. Under what circumstances might you claim exemption from withholding?

   ____

   ____

5. A single person making $240 weekly and claiming 1 allowance would have $13 withheld for income taxes. A married person making $240 weekly and claiming 1 allowance would have $3 withheld. Do you think this is fair? Why or why not?

   ____

   ____

Note: The figure for married persons is contained in a different table on IRS Publication 15, page 40.

Activity 6-6   Employment Terminology

Fill in the correct word(s) in the spaces provided.

1. The state of feeling worried or uneasy: _ _ _ _ _ _ _ _

2. Program provided in many organizations for new employees:

   _ _ _ _ _ _ _ _ _ _ _ _ _ _

3. The form most commonly filled out by new employees: _ _

4. The power or rank to give orders and make assignments to others:

   _ _ _ _ _ _ _ _ _ _

5. The duty to follow an order or carry out an assignment:

   _ _ _ _ _ _ _ _ _ _ _ _ _ _

6. Shows the flow of authority and responsibility in a company:

   _ _ _ _ _ _ _ _ _ _ _ _ _ _ _ _

7. Assigns a task or responsibility to others: _ _ _ _ _ _ _ _ _ _

8. Entry-level employees usually have a lot of _ _ _ _ _ _ _ _ _ _ _ _ _ _ _ _ _

   and little or no _ _ _ _ _ _ _ _ _ _

9. Answering to a supervisor: _ _ _ _ _ _ _ _ _ _ _ _

   _ _ _ _ _ _ _ _

10. This is based on rank or the chain of command: _ _ _ _ _ _ _

    _ _ _ _ _ _ _ _

11. This usually involves working for a specific person for a short time or for a certain
    assignment:

    _ _ _ _ _ _ _ _ _ _ _ _ _ _ _ _ _ _ _

12. A mood or spirit, such as the attitude and emotion of employees: _ _ _ _ _ _ _

13. A booklet that explains company policies and rules:

    _ _ _ _ _ _ _ _ _ _ _ _ _ _

14. One place where you might find policies and rules: _ _ _ _ _ _ _

    _ _ _ _ _ _ _

15. To pay back money already spent: _ _ _ _ _ _ _ _ _ _ _

16. The legal right to be notified of a complaint against you and to state your case or point
    of view before a decision is made: _ _ _ _ _ _ _ _ _ _ _ _

17. A trial period during which one's performance is observed and evaluated:

    _ _ _ _ _ _ _ _ _ _

18. Boss: _ _ _ _ _ _ _ _ _ _ _

19. Something you should ask your boss for: _ _ _ _ _ _ _ _ _ _

20. Something you should not ask your boss for: _ _ _ _ _ _ _ _ _

    _ _ _ _ _ _ _ _

21. Tax exemptions you are entitled to claim: _ _ _ _ _ _ _ _ _ _ _ _

22. Not required to pay taxes: _ _ _ _ _ _ _ _

Chapter 7 Expectations of Employers

7-1 Job Performance and Attitudes

Activity 7-1 **Cost of Lost Production**
Objective: To recognize the extent of financial losses incurred by employers when workers waste time on the job

Activity 7-2 **Expectations of Employers**
Objective: To identify the term or concept associated with various employer expectations regarding job performance, work habits, and attitudes

7-2 Grooming, Appearance, and Proper Dress

Activity 7-3 **Hairstyling and Hair Care**
Objective: To recognize that choice of a hairstyle may be based on one's facial features and hair characteristics

Activity 7-4 **Personal Hygiene**
Objective: To name terms and concepts associated with personal hygiene

Activity 7-5 **Dressing for the Job**
Objective: To recognize that jobs have different dress requirements

7-3 Rate Work Behavior

Activity 7-6 **Rating Work Behavior**
Objective: To rate and analyze your performance on the job

Activity 7-1   Cost of Lost Production

When you are late to work, leave early, or "goof off," it costs the company money. Suppose that you earn $8.50 an hour and work 250 days a year. You waste 10 minutes a day. The cost of lost production (CLP) can be computed by the following formula. The production cost is figured at 2 times the hourly rate. It may be more or less depending on the actual company involved.

$$CLP = \text{production cost} \times \text{hours lost} \times \text{days worked}$$

$$CLP = \$17.00 \times \frac{10}{60} \times 250$$

$$CLP = \$17.00 \times 0.17 \times 250$$

$$CLP = \$722.50$$

Problem: Assume that Richard earns $7.60 an hour and works 250 days a year. He is 5 minutes late to work, leaves 5 minutes early, and takes 5 extra minutes at lunch. Answer these questions.

1. How much does Richard cost the company each year in lost production? _________________

2. Richard is not alone; there are 20 more employees in the company just like him. How much do all of them cost the company per year?

   ____

3. Richard is 30 minutes late one morning. He works in a group with 5 other workers who earn the same wage as he does. The group cannot do anything until he arrives. How much does it cost the company to have 6 people waste 30 minutes of production time?

   ____

4. Richard was looking forward to a fat year-end bonus. However, the boss said that production was down during the year and there would be no bonuses. Richard and his buddies feel that the company cheated them out of their bonuses. What is your opinion?

   ____

   ____

   ____

   ____

5. Many companies dock employees for being late. Do you think this is fair? Why or why not?

   ____

   ____

   ____

   ____

                                        Chapter 7 Expectations of Employers

Activity 7-2   Expectations of Employers

Complete the following crossword puzzle by identifying the correct terms having to do with job performance, work habits, and attitudes.

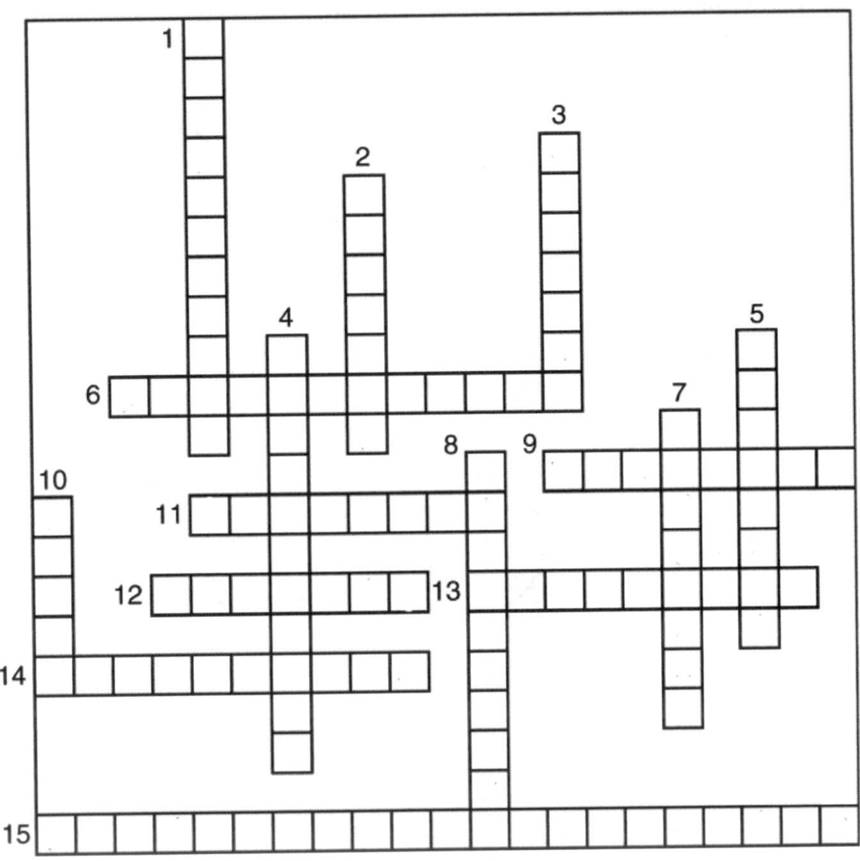

ACROSS

6. Worker output

9. Showing adult behavior

11. A feeling of excitement and involvement

12. Believing in and being devoted to something

13. Tools and machines

14. Eagerness or a strong interest in something

15. The process of judging how well an employee is doing on the job (2 words)

DOWN

1. Getting along with others

2. Not stealing or cheating

3. ______ of work; how well a job is performed

4. Being on time

5. Result of lack of safety consciousness

7. Thinking about a problem and making the right decision

8. Being at work when you are supposed to

10. A feeling of satisfaction with what you or someone you know has accomplished or possesses

Chapter 7 Expectations of Employers

Activity 7-3   Hairstyling and Hair Care

You should choose a hairstyle that goes well with your facial features and hair characteristics.
Place a check in the space corresponding to your primary facial shape. Also check all of the
hair characteristics that apply to you.

Facial Shape

_____________________ Oval

Hair Characteristics

_____________________ Thick

_____________________ Fine or limp

_____________________ Coarse

_____________________ Long

_____________________ Curly

_____________________ Dry

_____________________ Oily

_____________________ Round

_____________________ Split or dry ends

Dandruff

_____________________ Square

_____________________ Heart-shaped

Based on your facial shape, what would be a good hairstyle for you?

____

____

____

Based on your characteristics, what type of care does your hair require?

____

____

____

Chapter 7 Expectations of Employers

Activity 7-4   Personal Hygiene

A good appearance on the job begins with personal hygiene. Test how much you know about hygiene by matching the phrase in the right column with the correct term on the left. Not all answers are in the textbook.

_______ 1. Personal hygiene   a. Black-tipped plug clogging a pore

_______ 2. Pores   b. Fluid secreted by sweat glands

_______ 3. Deodorant   c. Care of teeth and gums

_______ 4. Perspiration   d. Germs that cause odor

_______ 5. Bacteria   e. Bad breath

_______ 6. Acne   f. Keeping one's body clean and healthy

_______ 7. Hormones   g. Excess flaking of dead skin on scalp

_______ 8. Blackhead   h. Openings in skin

_______ 9. Pimple   i. Tooth decay

_______ 10. Hair follicles   j. Product used to control underarm perspiration odor

_______ 11. Dandruff   k. Common skin condition

_______ 12. Dermatologist   l. Infected pore

_______ 13. Oral hygiene   m. Small cavities in skin containing growing hair and oil-secreting glands

_______ 14. Cavities   n. Body chemicals that regulate or stimulate functions; e.g., that stimulate glands to produce oil

_______ 15. Halitosis   o. Doctor who treats skin problems

What hygiene or personal care considerations are particularly important in the occupation for which you are training or that you hope to follow?

____

____

____

____

____

____

Chapter 7 Expectations of Employers

Activity 7-5   Dressing for the Job

Dressing appropriately for a job may involve more than simply looking good. Rate the following factors in terms of how important they are in your job (or a job of interest).

Type of job: ____

	Very Important	Important	Of Little Importance	Not Important
Appearance	_________	_________	_________	_________
Comfort	_________	_________	_________	_________
Protection	_________	_________	_________	_________
Sanitation	_________	_________	_________	_________
Durability	_________	_________	_________	_________

Describe the attire of a worker in the above type of job who would be considered appropriately dressed.

____

____

____

____

Give examples of types of jobs in which each of the following dress factors are of prime importance.

Appearance: ____

____

Comfort: ____

____

Protection: ____

____

Sanitation: ____

____

Durability: ____

____

   Chapter 7 Expectations of Employers

Activity 7-6   Rating Work Behavior

How well are you doing in your job? Rate yourself on these ten items having to do with job performance, work habits, and attitudes. Circle the number that corresponds to your rating in each area. If you do not have a job, rate your behavior in terms of your schoolwork.

	Excellent	Very Good	Average	Fair	Poor
1. Productivity	5	4	3	2	1
2. Quality of work	5	4	3	2	1
3. Judgment	5	4	3	2	1
4. Safety consciousness	5	4	3	2	1
5. Care of equipment	5	4	3	2	1
6. Attendance and punctuality	5	4	3	2	1
7. Cooperation	5	4	3	2	1
8. Interest and enthusiasm	5	4	3	2	1
9. Honesty	5	4	3	2	1
10. Loyalty	5	4	3	2	1

After you have rated yourself, show your ratings to your job supervisor or teacher. Are there areas in which you have rated yourself too low?

____

____

Are there areas in which you have rated yourself too high?

____

____

What are your weakest areas? What can you do to improve in these areas?

____

____

____

____

____

Chapter 7 Expectations of Employers

Chapter 8 Worker Rights and Protections

8-1 Duties of Employers

Activity 8-1 **Labor-Management Relations**
Objective: To recognize the position of each party on a representative labor-management issue

Activity 8-2 **Equal Employment Opportunity**
Objective: To name the term or concept associated with various equal opportunity principles and practices

8-2 Worker Safety and Health

Activity 8-3 **Worker Rights and Protections**
Objective: To summarize the requirements regarding fair employment practices for the state in which you live

8-3 Your Job Earnings and Paycheck

Activity 8-4 **Figuring Compensation**
Objective: To calculate various types of compensation

Activity 8-5 **Your Paycheck**
Objective: To figure earnings and deductions for a sample paycheck

8-4 Job Changes

Activity 8-6 **Letter of Resignation**
Objective: To write a sample letter of resignation

Activity 8-1   Labor-Management Relations

Investigate a recent strike or other labor-management disagreement in your community or state. Identify the main issue and explain the position of each party.

Issue: ____

____

____

Labor Position ⟵——————⟶ Management Position

_________________________ _________________________

_________________________ _________________________

_________________________ _________________________

_________________________ _________________________

_________________________ _________________________

_________________________ _________________________

_________________________ _________________________

_________________________ _________________________

Describe how the issue was finally resolved and what the terms of the settlement were.

____

____

____

Did either party win, or was the outcome a compromise? Explain.

____

____

____

____

Chapter 8 Worker Rights and Protections

Activity 8-2   Equal Employment Opportunity

Complete the following word puzzle by filling in the correct terms.

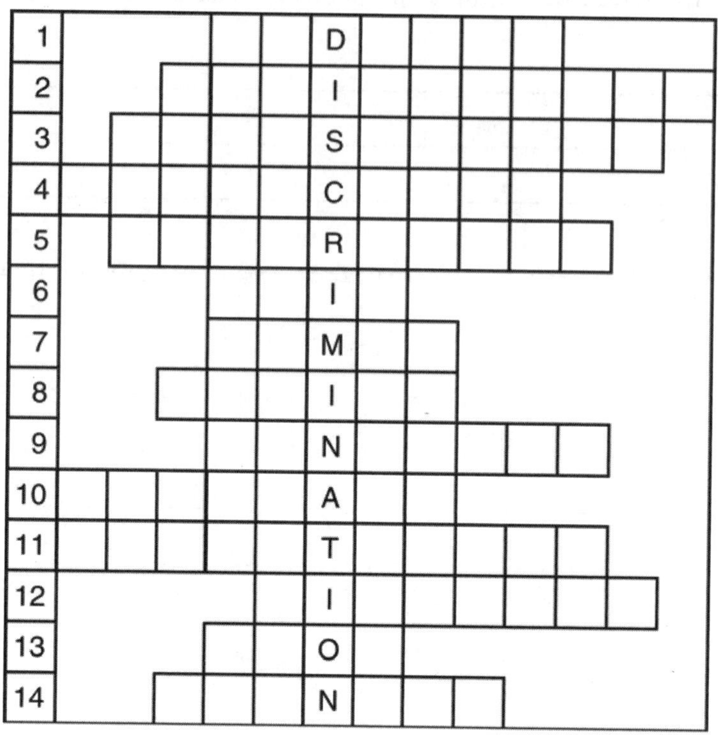

1. Level of government that has acted to protect equal employment opportunity

2. Action that is designed to remedy past discrimination

3. Laws that have been passed, such as those to protect equal employment opportunity

4. Something that equal employment opportunity legislation provides

5. Groups that have been discriminated against

6. Equal treatment

7. Group that has been discriminated against because of its sex

8. __________ and Medical Leave Act

9. The legislative body that passes federal laws

10. Individuals who served in the Armed Forces and who are covered by affirmative action

11. Something provided by equal employment practices

12. Group for whom equal employment opportunity was extended in 1973

13. Federal agency that enforces equal employment opportunity legislation

14. Former President of the United States who first promoted affirmative action

                                                          Chapter 8 Worker Rights and Protections

Activity 8-3 Worker Rights and Protections

Use what you have learned in this chapter about worker rights and protections to answer the following questions. You will need to research state and federal laws for some questions.

1. Jaime works at a large aircraft engine plant. He and his wife are planning to adopt a six-year-old girl. Jaime would like to have some time off to be with his new daughter. Is Jaime entitled to leave under state or federal law? Write down the name of the law with the higher standard (state or federal), how much leave Jaime is entitled to, and any conditions (such as whether the leave is paid or unpaid).

____

____

____

2. Milly is one of five female machine operators at a factory. She and the other women have learned that they are being paid substantially less than male factory operators who perform the same kind of work. The factory is not a union shop. Milly has followed her company's procedures for addressing the problem without success. What should she do next?

____

____

____

____

3. Wendy is a new employee at an auto collision repair shop. Today she is given a new kind of solvent to use to clean car parts before painting. Wendy reads the directions and sees that hazardous fumes can be created if the solvent is not properly prepared. She points this out to the more experienced coworker she's been assigned to work with. He tells her not to worry about it and starts to mix the solvent the way it has always been done. What should Wendy do?

____

4. Josefina is a work experience student working at a restaurant as a chef's assistant. She has noticed that one of the cooks frequently fails to wash her hands between food preparation steps, which include handling raw meat. What should Josefina do?

____

____

Activity 8-4   Figuring Compensation

Figure the following problems related to work compensation.

1. Pete earns $8.35 an hour for a $37\frac{1}{2}$-hour week. How much does he earn per week? ____________ Per month? ____________

2. Wilma makes $415 per week. She works 50 weeks and gets paid for a 2-week vacation. How much is her annual pay? ____________

3. Carl receives $9.10 an hour for the first 40 hours he works and time and a half for overtime. If he works 45 hours, how much does he earn for the week? ____________

4. Evan is paid $790 biweekly. How much does he make per week? ____________ Per month? ____________

5. Michael receives a monthly salary of $2,500 plus a commission of 2% of total orders written. If his orders for the month were $34,000, what is his total pay? ____________

6. Lisa sold a condominium for $152,000. The commission is 6%. She gets 3% and the buyer's broker gets 3%. How much commission did Lisa earn on the sale? ____________

7. Kim works from 6 to 11 on Friday and Saturday evenings at Lombardi's Italian Restaurant. She gets $7.75 an hour plus tips. Her tips were $32.35 on Friday and $40.10 on Saturday. How much did she earn for the 2 nights' work? ____________ How much did she average per hour? ____________

8. Roger is a teacher who earns $42,000 for the 9-month school year. However, his salary is paid out in 12 monthly installments. How much does he get per month? ____________

9. Doug packs boxes at the rate of $.75 per box. He averages 12 boxes per hour. How much does he earn in an 8-hour day? ____________

10. Brenda earned $32,000 last year and received a 15% year-end bonus. What were her total earnings? ____________

Chapter 8 Worker Rights and Protections

Activity 8-5 Your Paycheck

Refer to the sample pay statement and answer the following questions as if you are the payee.

EMPLOYEE'S PAY STATEMENT
DETACH AND RETAIN FOR YOUR RECORDS

HOURS	EARNINGS			FEDERAL INC TAX	FICA	STATE INC TAX	INSURANCE	NET PAY
	REG	OVERTIME	TOTAL					
45	350.00	66.00	416.00	37.00	31.82	10.00	10.94	326.24

PEN-MART, INC. **PAYROLL CHECK** 01462

January 10, 20 -- ____

PAY TO THE ORDER OF ___ **Jill Yount** ___ $ 326.24

Three hundred twenty-six and $\frac{24}{100}$ ___ DOLLARS

First City Bank
MIDDLETON, VERMONT

Jay Whitney
TREASURER

1. How many hours did you work this pay period? ____________

2. What was your regular pay? ____________ Overtime pay? ____________

3. What was the amount of your gross earnings? ____________

4. How much was withheld for federal income tax? ____________

    State income tax? ____________

5. How much was deducted for Social Security tax? ____________

6. What was the amount withheld for insurance? ____________

7. What were the total deductions for this pay period? ____________

8. What percent of your gross pay was withheld? ____________

9. If you work the same number of hours for the next three weeks, what will be your total

    net pay for the month? ____________

10. Why is it important to check your pay statement for accuracy and keep it for your records?

    ____

    ____

Chapter 8 Worker Rights and Protections

Activity 8-6   Letter of Resignation

Assume that you have been employed as a work experience education student/learner at Solar Tech, Inc., 4 Main St., Yuma, AZ 85364-1218. At the end of the school year, you are going to enter the Army. Write an appropriate letter of resignation to your supervisor, Ms. Kim Lee.

____

____

____

____

____

____

Dear ___________________________

____

____

____

____

____

____

____

____

____

Sincerely

____

     Chapter 8 Worker Rights and Protections

Chapter 9   Workplace Communication

9-1   Listen and Speak

9-2   Read and Write

9-3   Effective Communication and Group Participation

9-4   Bosses, Coworkers, and Customers

Activity 9-1   Effective Listening

Give an example of each of the following barriers to effective listening. Try to use an example related to a job or school situation.

Distraction: ____

____

____

____

Prejudging: ____

____

____

____

Overstimulation: ____

____

____

____

Partial listening: ____

____

____

____

Have you ever been involved in an accident or other serious situation because of not listening to what you were told? Describe such an incident or give an example that you are familiar with.

____

____

____

____

____

____

                                                    Chapter 9 Workplace Communication

Activity 9-2   Correcting a Business Form

Jenny works for a roofing company. Yesterday she turned in the following job work order. What would you think of it if you were her supervisor or the customer? List any suggestions you have for Jenny at the bottom of the page. Also, list anything about the form that she did well.

<table>
<tr><td colspan="2" align="center">JOB WORK ORDER
No. 4875</td></tr>
<tr><td>CUSTOMER
Ramona Rivera</td><td>DATE OF ORDER
5/22/—</td></tr>
<tr><td colspan="2">STREET ADDRESS
6231 Park</td></tr>
<tr><td colspan="2">CITY
Chula Vista</td></tr>
<tr><td>TELEPHONE: WORK
555-0125</td><td>HOME</td></tr>
<tr><td>STARTING DATE</td><td>DATE COMPLETED
5/27</td></tr>
<tr><td colspan="2">DESCRIPTION OF WORK
Front entry roof redone. Replaced the bad wood. Repaint the brick joints on right side chimney & flash lower right side chimney upper right side to. The gutters was cleaned & I painted the roof metal work. Found a lose soffit & renailed it. Replaced some rotted wood on front rake, it was the right side. Fixed hole behind chimney & 10 ft of downspout</td></tr>
<tr><td>PAID BY
☐ Cash
☐ Credit Card
☐ Bill
☐ Check No. _______</td><td>MATERIALS
LABOR
TAX
TOTAL   3579.86</td></tr>
<tr><td>SERVICE REP NO.
Jenny</td><td>CUSTOMER'S SIGNATURE
Ramona Rivera</td></tr>
</table>

____

____

____

____

Chapter 9 Workplace Communication

Activity 9-3   Writing an Email

Assume that you work in the Shipping Department and have discovered several errors on an invoice that is to be sent out along with a carton of goods. Write an email to Terry Foster in the Accounting Department telling him of your discovery and asking him whether to go ahead and ship the goods.

EMAIL

TO: ____________________________________

FROM: __________________________________

DATE: __________________________________

SUBJECT: _______________________________

____

____

____

____

____

____

____

____

____

____

____

____

____

____

                                          Chapter 9 Workplace Communication

Activity 9-4   Communication Skills

Complete the following crossword puzzle by identifying the correct terms having to do with communication skills and processes.

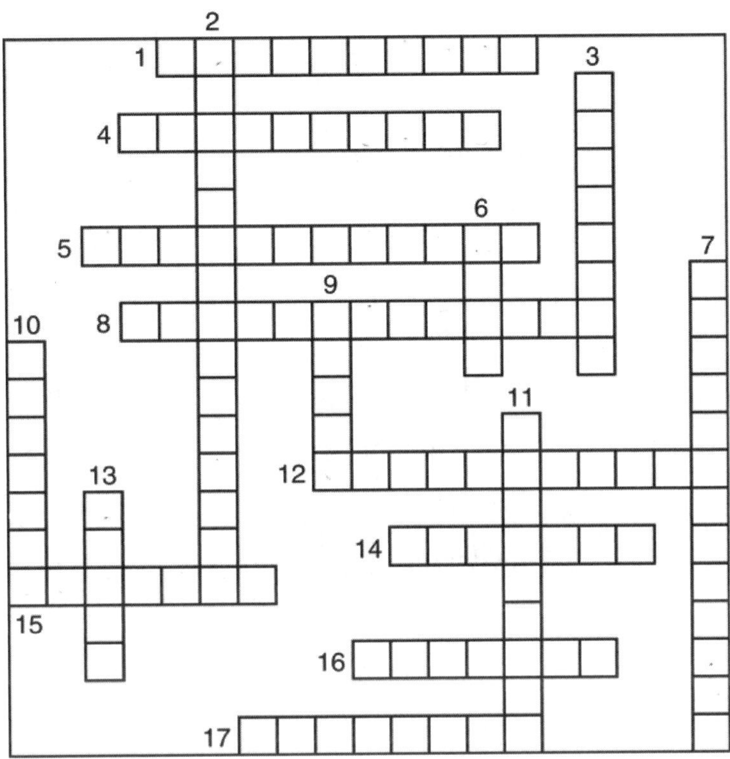

ACROSS

1. The total of all the words you know
4. An example of this is coming to a conclusion before you have heard any or all of the facts
5. Things that interfere with listening
8. Sending information, ideas, or feelings from one person to another
12. How distinctly or clearly one speaks
14. Written language
15. One way to visually receive information
16. The primary language used in the United States
17. Before sending a message composed on software, you should run the _____ checker.

DOWN

2. An example of this is wanting to challenge what the speaker is saying and then missing the message
3. Oral communication
6. The most informal type of written business communication
7. The way in which words are spoken
9. A common distraction
10. A set of rules about correct speaking and writing
11. Receiving oral communication and other sounds
13. This is becoming the preferred form of personal and business communication.

Activity 9-5   Spelling and Grammar

Half of the following words are misspelled. Underline the 15 incorrect words. For each incorrect word, write the correctly spelled word on the line to the right.

accesible _______________	equipped _______________	ninty _______________
achievement _______________	excillent _______________	originel _______________
apparant _______________	fascinate _______________	precede _______________
beginner _______________	fourty _______________	proceed _______________
business _______________	greevance _______________	receipt _______________
changable _______________	hoping _______________	refering _______________
committ _______________	imediately _______________	sense _______________
consistent _______________	independent _______________	transfered _______________
decision _______________	license _______________	usefull _______________
desparete _______________	medacine _______________	weird _______________

Circle and then correct the grammatical error in each of the following sentences.

1. I have looked for the wrench, but it ain't here. _______________________________

2. Was you aware of the problem? _______________________________

3. It don't seem like quitting time. _______________________________

4. He might of left the paperwork here. _______________________________

5. I done that same job yesterday. _______________________________

6. She brung the new parts for us to see. _______________________________

7. I seen them unload the new machine. _______________________________

8. This here manual explains how to do it. _______________________________

9. I do not have nothing to lose. _______________________________

10. We could not scarcely see a thing. _______________________________

11. The application of robots are expanding rapidly. _______________________________

12. The pen, pad, and calculator is all here. _______________________________

     Chapter 9 Workplace Communication

Activity 9-6   Working in Groups

1. List two good experiences that you have had working in groups. Explain why they were good experiences. _______________________________________

____

____

____

2. List two bad experiences that you have had working in groups. Explain why they were bad experiences. _______________________________________

____

____

3. Pages 221–222 of the text give guidelines for working effectively in a group. List two additional suggestions. _______________________________________

____

____

4. In a magazine or newspaper or on the Internet, find an article on working in groups. Print or copy the article, read it, highlight important points, and summarize it.

____

____

____

____

____

____

____

Activity 9-7   Interpersonal Relations

Identify and describe an interpersonal relations problem that you have had with the following individuals. Then explain how the problem might have been avoided by different behavior on your part.

With a family member

1. Problem: ____

____

____

2. How avoided: ____

____

____

____

With an employer (or teacher)

3. Problem: ____

____

____

4. How avoided: ____

____

____

____

With a coworker (or fellow student)

5. Problem: ____

____

____

6. How avoided: ____

____

____

____

   Chapter 9 Workplace Communication

Activity 9-8   Customer Relations

Assume that you are working in a retail store. Explain how you should or might respond to each of these situations.

1. A customer you have never seen before comes into the store _______________________

____

____

____

2. A frequent, well-known customer comes into the store _________________________

____

____

____

3. A customer just wants to look around ____

____

____

____

4. A customer returns a product after getting home and deciding that he does not like it

____

____

____

5. A customer returns a defective product and is irate because it does not work __________

____

____

____

6. A customer seems intent on wanting to buy an article of clothing that does not fit right

or look good on her ____

____

____

____

(Continued on next page)

Activity 9-8   Customer Relations

7. A customer claims you have charged him too much for a purchase ___________________

   ____

   ____

   ____

8. A customer asks you to suggest a gift item for someone "just your size" _____________

   ____

   ____

   ____

9. You observe a customer stealing something ____________________________________

   ____

   ____

   ____

10. A customer is about to leave the store without having bought anything _____________

   ____

   ____

   ____

11. A customer is preparing to pay for an item that is priced $10 too low _______________

   ____

   ____

   ____

12. A customer is about to buy a $200 item that is going to be marked down 30 percent

   tomorrow ____

   ____

   ____

   ____

                                        Chapter 9 Workplace Communication

Activity 9-9   Special Human Relations Skills

Some occupations require special human relations skills beyond those explained in Chapter 9. They may involve dealing with circumstances such as accident or illness, danger, death, uncooperative behavior, unwelcome or distressing news, and violence. For each occupation below, provide an example of a situation requiring special human relations skills.

Attorney: ____

____

Dentist: ____

____

Flight attendant: ____

____

High school principal: _____________________________________

____

Hotel counter clerk: ______________________________________

____

Insurance agent: ____

____

911 dispatcher: ____

____

Physical therapist: ____

____

Police officer: ____

____

Public relations specialist: _________________________________

____

Undertaker: ____

____

Veterinarian: ____

____

Chapter 10   Math and Measurement Skills

10-1   Basic Math

Activity 10-1   **Basic Math**
Objective: To compute the answer to various business math problems

10-2   Basic Measurement

Activity 10-2   **Basic Measurement**
Objective: To compute the answer to various measurement problems

Activity 10-3   **Math and Measurement Terminology**
Objective: To name terms and concepts associated with math and measurement

Activity 10-1   Basic Math

Complete the following business math problems. Place your answers in the boxes provided.
Use the space at the bottom of each page to make computations if you need it.

Total purchase amount

1.

$8 \times \$ .99 = \$$ __________

$4 \times\ \ .35 = \$$ __________

$6 \times\ 1.43 = \$$ __________

$\$$ [____]

2.

$7 \times \$ 3.49 = \$$ __________

$12 \times\ \ \ \ .95 = \$$ __________

$6 \times\ 12.63 = \$$ __________

$\$$ [____]

3.

$24 \times \$ 7.50 = \$$ __________

$30 \times\ 18.90 = \$$ __________

$22 \times\ 13.27 = \$$ __________

$9 \times\ \ \ 8.07 = \$$ __________

$14 \times\ 21.65 = \$$ __________

$\$$ [____]

Trade discount

	4.	**5.**	**6.**	**7.**
List price:	$175.00	$1,470.00	$820.00	$79.00
% discount:	25%	40%	33%	20%
Discount:	$ [ ]	$ [ ]	$ [ ]	$ [ ]
Net purchase price:	$ [ ]	$ [ ]	$ [ ]	$ [ ]

Markup

	8.	**9.**		**10.**	**11.**
Selling price:	$96.00	$250.00	Cost price:	$50.00	$115.00
Cost price:	$60.00	$200.00	% markup:	30%	25%
Markup:	$ [ ]	$ [ ]	Markup:	$ [ ]	$ [ ]
% markup:	[ ] %	[ ] %	Selling price:	$ [ ]	$ [ ]

(Continued on next page)

Activity 10-1   Basic Math

Sales tax	12.	13.	14.	15.
Purchase price:	$48.00	$135.00	$260.00	$94.00
% sales tax:	5%	4%	3.5%	2%
Sales tax:	$	$	$	$
Total amount:	$	$	$	$

Markdown	16.	17.	18.	19.
Original price:	$ 60.00	$165.00	$89.50	$324.00
% markdown:	25%	50%	30%	40%
Markdown:	$	$	$	$
Sale price:	$	$	$	$

                                    Chapter 10 Math and Measurement Skills

Activity 10-2   Basic Measurement

Complete the following problems. Carry your answers to two decimal places. Place them in the spaces provided.

Shapes and Dimensions

1. What is the name of each of these common geometric shapes?

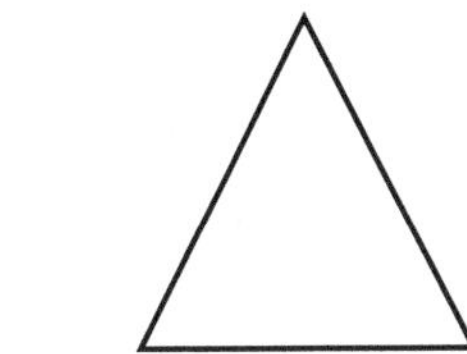      

A. ____________   B ____________   C. ____________

2. What three main dimensions of a circle are shown below?

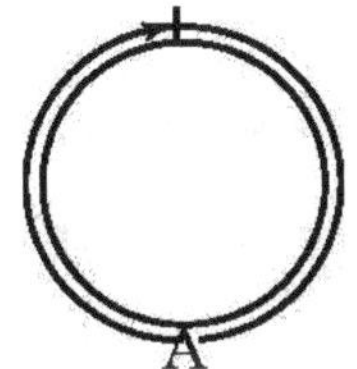   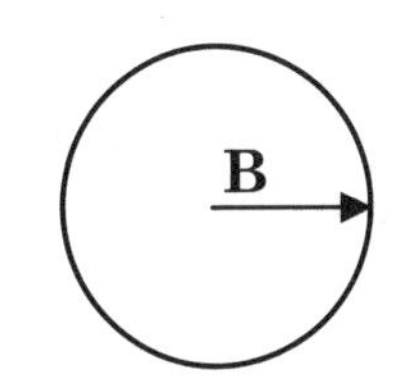   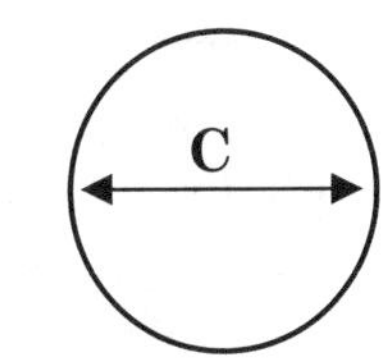

A. ____________   B. ____________   C. ____________

Perimeter

3. What is the perimeter of a triangle that is 7.5 feet on each side? ____________

4. A carpenter is putting baseboard around a room that is 12 feet long and 10 feet wide. The room has 3 doorways, each 3 feet wide. How many linear feet of molding are needed?

   ____

5. Suppose that you must enclose an equipment yard with fencing and have 48 feet of fencing. One side of the rectangular yard will be 6 feet. What will be the dimensions of the equipment yard?

   ____

6. What is the circumference in feet of a circle that has a diameter of 3 feet 3 inches?

   ____

7. What is the radius of a circle that has a circumference of 12.56 feet? ____________

Area

8. What is the area in square feet of a room 22 feet 3 inches long and 12 feet wide?

   ____

9. What is the length of a room that contains 252 square feet and is 18 feet wide?

   ____

(Continued on next page)

Chapter 10 Math and Measurement Skills

95

Activity 10-2   Basic Measurement

10. You need to carpet a room that measures 12 × 21 feet. Carpeting costs $11.95 a square yard. How much will the carpet cost?

    ____

11. What is the area in square inches of a circle that has a diameter of 2 feet 4 inches?

    ____

12. What is the radius in feet of a circle that contains 78.5 square feet? ___________________

Volume

13. What is the volume in cubic inches of a rectangular solid that is 6 feet long, 16 inches high, and 3 feet 6 inches wide?

    ____

14. A rectangular storage bin measures 18 × 12 × 12 feet. If a struck bushel is equal to 1.24 cubic feet, how many struck bushels of grain would it hold?

    ____

15. How many cubic yards of concrete would be required to pour a 6-inch concrete slab that measures 32 × 18 feet?

    ____

Metric

16. Express 100 yards in meters. ___________________

17. If a machine part measures 28 centimeters in length, how long is the part in inches?

    ____

18. How many centimeters are there in 3 feet? ___________________

19. Express 130 pounds in kilograms. ___________________

20. A crate weighs 20,000 kilograms. How many pounds does it weigh? ___________________

21. A room that is 12 feet on each side contains how many cubic meters? ___________________

22. If a truck takes 38 liters to fill, how many gallons does this equal? ___________________

   Chapter 10 Math and Measurement Skills

Activity 10-3   Math and Measurement Terminology

Fill in the correct word(s) in the spaces provided.

1. Common uses of arithmetic at work: _ _ _ _ _ _ _ _   _ _ _ _ _

2. The price of one item: _ _ _ _

3. A bill for goods: _ _ _ _ _ _ _ _

4. A deduction from the catalog (list) price of an item:

   _ _ _ _ _   _ _ _ _ _ _ _ _ _

5. These state the time limit within which the buyer must pay: _ _ _ _ _ _

6. A reduction in price offered to encourage early payment:

   _ _ _ _   _ _ _ _ _ _ _ _

7. The price a retailer pays for goods: _ _ _ _ _

8. An amount added by the retailer to the cost price: _ _ _ _ _ _ _

9. Tax added to the purchase price of goods: _ _ _ _ _ _

10. A reduction in the selling price of a product: _ _ _ _ _ _ _ _ _ _

11. The act of determining "how much": _ _ _ _ _ _ _ _ _ _ _ _

12. The distance around an object: _ _ _ _ _ _ _ _ _

13. The perimeter of a circle: _ _ _ _ _ _ _ _ _ _ _ _ _ _

14. One-half the diameter of a circle: _ _ _ _ _ _

15. The number of square units of space on the surface of a figure enclosed by the perimeter:

    _ _ _ _

16. The formula for determining the area of a rectangle:

    _ _ _ _ _ _   ×   _ _ _ _ _

17. The constant used in the formula to find the area of a circle: _ . _ _

18. Length, width, and height: _ _ _ _ _ _ _ _ _ _ _

19. A number that has been multiplied by itself: _ _ _ _ _ _ _ _

20. The amount of space an object takes up: _ _ _ _ _ _ _

21. The measure used to express the volume of rectangular objects: _ _ _ _ _ _

22. The process of changing from one unit of measure to another:

    _ _ _ _ _ _ _ _ _ _ _

23. The most widely used system of measurement: _ _ _ _ _ _ _ _

24 The basic unit of measure in the metric system: _ _ _ _ _ _

25. The basic unit of weight in the metric system: _ _ _ _ _

Chapter 11   Health and Safety

11-1   Nutrition and Diet

11-2   Stress and Physical Fitness

11-3   Accidents and Personal Safety

11-4   Natural Disasters and Public Safety

Activity 11-1   Calorie Counting

Keep track of everything you eat and drink (except water) for one day. List the foods and beverages. Record the number of calories for each item (for example, 6-oz orange juice, 83).

Breakfast	Lunch	Dinner	Snacks
_______________	_______________	_______________	_______________
_______________	_______________	_______________	_______________
_______________	_______________	_______________	_______________
_______________	_______________	_______________	_______________
_______________	_______________	_______________	_______________
_______________	_______________	_______________	_______________
_______________	_______________	_______________	_______________

Calories __________   Calories __________   Calories __________   Calories __________

1. How many total calories did you consume for the entire period? ____________________

2. What is your approximate caloric need, based on guidelines provided on page 260 of your text? For more specific information, consult the following website:

   www.freedieting.com/tools/calorie_calculator.htm ____________________

3. Is your calorie intake for the day above or below your needs? ____________________

4. By how much? ____________________

5. What percent of your calorie intake is composed of snack items?

   (snack calories ÷ total calories × 100) ____________________

6. Let us assume that you want to reduce your caloric intake. List five food or drink items (and their calories) that you could substitute for five of the high-calorie items listed.

   a. ____________________ instead of ____________________

   b. ____________________ instead of ____________________

   c. ____________________ instead of ____________________

   d. ____________________ instead of ____________________

   e. ____________________ instead of ____________________

Chapter 11 Health and Safety

Activity 11-2   Calorie Expenditure

This table lists the approximate number of calories per hour it takes to perform four types of activities. (The actual calories for individuals will vary.) Use it to answer the questions.

Activity Type	Calories	Examples
Light	105	Tasks done while sitting, standing, or walking slowly, such as reading, watching TV, working at a computer, grooming, washing dishes, doing laundry, sweeping, or shopping
Moderate	280	Carpentry, electrical work, stocking shelves, gardening, carrying a child, washing a car, walking (2.5–4.5 miles per hour), bike riding (leisurely), low-impact aerobics, water aerobics, bowling, or golf
Vigorous	420	Outside construction, shoveling snow, race walking, bike riding (10–11.9 mph), swimming laps (slowly), aerobic dancing, basketball, or tennis (doubles)
Strenuous	700	Carrying heavy loads, running, bike riding (>12 mph), swimming laps (moderate to vigorous), roller skating, tennis (singles)

1. About how many calories will be consumed in watching television for 3 hours? _________

2. If it takes you 2 hours to wash your car, how many calories will you consume? _________

3. Walking at 3 mph will consume how many more calories per hour than slow walking? ______

4. It takes about 3,500 calories to lose 1 pound of stored body fat. If you walk at 2.5 mph for 30 minutes a day, about how long will it take to lose 1 pound? ____________ About how many pounds will you lose in 6 months? ______

5. If, in addition to walking 2.5 mph for 30 minutes a day, you reduce your daily calorie intake by 365 (10 french fries and a 12-oz root beer), about how long will it take you to lose 1 pound? _________ About how many pounds will you lose in 6 months? ______

6. If you reduce your calorie intake by 500 and increase your calorie use by 500 a day, about how long will it take you to lose a pound? __________

7. If you want to lose weight, what two approaches are recommended? __________________
____

8. If you go on a diet, what is the minimum number of calories you should maintain? ______
Why? ____

Activity 11-3   Learning to Relax

Use your textbook, an encyclopedia, or the Web as required to answer these questions.

1. How do you react to stress? _________________________________

____

2. What is meant by the term *meditation*? _____________________

____

____

3. What types of bodily changes can be produced by meditation? _______________________

____

____

Try this simple relaxation technique (meditation). Sit or lie in a comfortable position in a quiet place where you will not be disturbed. Close your eyes, and silently repeat the word "one" over and over for a period of 10–20 minutes. Block out any other thoughts and concentrate on establishing a rhythmic pattern. Try not to move any muscles.

4. How do you feel after meditating? Describe any feelings or bodily changes that you noticed

   while meditating. ____

____

____

____

____

5. What do you do to manage stress? _________________________

____

____

____

6. Why is it important to be able to control stress? _______________________

____

____

Chapter 11 Health and Safety

Activity 11-4   Healthstyle Self-rating

Circle the number corresponding to the answer that best describes your behavior
(Almost Always, Sometimes, Almost Never).

	Almost Always	Some-times	Almost Never
EATING HABITS			
1. I eat a variety of foods each day, including fruit, vegetables, whole-grain breads and cereals, and dairy products.	4	1	0
2. I limit the amount of fat, saturated fat, and cholesterol I eat (fat on meat, eggs, butter, etc.).	2	1	0
3. I limit the amount of salt I eat.	2	1	0
4. I avoid eating too much sugar.	2	1	0
Eating Habits Score:			
EXERCISE/FITNESS			
1. I maintain my recommended weight.	3	1	0
2. I exercise for at least 30 minutes at least three times a week.	3	1	0
3. I do stretching and flexibility exercises for 15 to 30 minutes at least three times a week.	2	1	0
4. I use part of my leisure time participating in physical activities that increase my level of fitness.	2	1	0
Exercise/Fitness Score:			
STRESS CONTROL			
1. I have a job or do other work that I enjoy.	2	1	0
2. I find it easy to relax and express my feelings freely.	2	1	0
3. I recognize early, and prepare for, events or situations likely to be stressful for me.	2	1	0
4. I have close friends, relatives, or others whom I can talk to about personal matters and call on for help.	2	1	0
5. I participate in group activities or hobbies that I enjoy.	2	1	0
Stress Control Score:			

(Continued on next page)

   Chapter 11 Health and Safety

Activity 11-4   Healthstyle Self-rating

	Almost Always	Some-times	Almost Never
SAFETY			
1. I wear a seat and shoulder belt while riding in a car	2	1	0
2. I avoid driving while under the influence of alcohol and other drugs.	2	1	0
3. I obey traffic rules and the speed limit when driving.	2	1	0
4. I am careful when using potentially harmful products or substances (such as household cleaners, poisons, and electrical devices).	2	1	0
5. I get at least 7 hours of sleep a night.	2	1	0
Safety Score:			

Interpret each section separately as follows:

10–9   **Excellent.** Your answers show that you are aware of the effect of this area on your health.
 8–6   **Good.** Your health practices are good, but there is room for improvement.
 5–3   **Poor.** Your health risks are showing.
 2–0   **Failing.** You may be taking serious and unnecessary risks with your health.

Where do you go from here? Start by asking yourself a few frank questions:

1. Am I really doing all I can to be as healthy as possible?   **Yes**   **No**

2. What steps can I take to be more healthful?

____

____

____

____

3. Am I willing to begin now?   **Yes**   **No**   If the answer is no, why not?

____

____

____

Adapted from *Healthstyle: A Self Test.* U.S. Department of Health and Human Services, 1981.

Chapter 11 Health and Safety   103

Activity 11-5   Fitness Tests

Perform each of the following five fitness tests. Have someone help you to keep time and to record information. Do not do the tests if you do not feel well or do not want to do them.

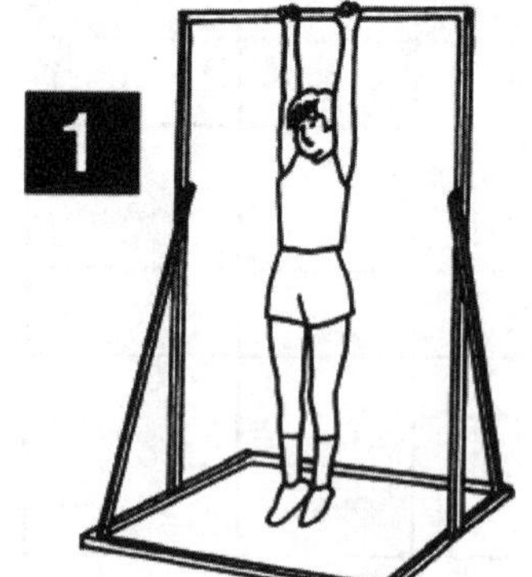

Arm Hang: Hang from the bar for as long as possible.

Your score in minutes and seconds: ___________________________

Sit & Reach: Reach forward as far as possible while sitting (measure from crotch to fingertips).

Your score in inches you can reach: ___________________________

Curl-ups: Do as many correct curl-ups as possible in one minute.

Your score in number of curl-ups: ___________________________

Push-ups: Do as many push-ups as possible in one minute. (Note different style for men and women.)

Your score in number of push-ups: ___________________________

Step Test: Step up and down on a 12-inch-high bench in rhythm for 3 minutes. Measure your heart rate after the exercise.

Your heartbeats per minute: ___________________________

(Continued on next page)

Chapter 11 Health and Safety

Activity 11-5   Fitness Tests

Interpret your performance using the chart that follows. Find out whether you deserve a gold, silver, or bronze rating.

	Rating	Arm Hang	Sit & Reach	Curl-ups	Push-ups	Step Test
Female	Gold	1:31+	23+	46+	46+	to 79
	Silver	:46–1:30	17–22	25–45	17–45	80–110
	Bronze	to :45	to 16	to 24	to 16	111+
Male	Gold	2:01+	22+	51+	51+	to 74
	Silver	1:00–2:00	13–21	30–50	25–50	75–100
	Bronze	to :59	to 12	to 29	to 24	101+

How would you describe your overall fitness level (excellent, good, average, or poor)?

____

If indicated, describe what you might do to improve your fitness level.

____

____

____

Reproduced from the National Fitness Foundation.

Chapter 11 Health and Safety

Activity 11-6   Preventing Accidents

What occupation are you currently preparing for or hoping to follow upon completing your education or training? ____

Name the five most common accidents involving this occupation. Then, explain how each type of accident can best be avoided.

1. ____

____

2. ____

____

3. ____

4. ____

5. ____

____

List as many different types of safety devices and equipment as you can think of that are used in your occupation.

____

____

____

____

____

____

____

____

____

Activity 11-7   Auto Safety Check Sheet

Use the following checklist to conduct a safety inspection of your car, the family car, or another vehicle.

Yes No BRAKES

☐ ☐ Stop car in 25 feet or less from 20 mph

☐ ☐ All four wheels take hold evenly.

☐ ☐ Take hold evenly before brake pedal is 1 inch from floor

☐ ☐ Emergency brake can hold car on any hill.

☐ ☐ Make no scratchy sound when applied

☐ ☐ Brake fluid clean and at proper level

HEADLIGHTS

☐ ☐ Aimed for maximum light on road and minimum glare

☐ ☐ Dimming switch and upper and lower beams in good working order

☐ ☐ Lenses clean and reflectors bright

REAR LIGHTS AND SIGNALS

☐ ☐ Bulbs burn—controls work

☐ ☐ Brakes operate stop light.

☐ ☐ Lenses clean, clear, and free of cracks

☐ ☐ Reflectors in good condition

TIRES

☐ ☐ Treads and sidewalls free from worn spots, cuts, and breaks

☐ ☐ Properly inflated

☐ ☐ Even wear shows wheel alignment OK and no tire rotation necessary

☐ ☐ Ample tread

REARVIEW MIRROR

☐ ☐ Clear, steady view of road behind

☐ ☐ Easily adjusted

(Continued on next page)

Activity 11-7   Auto Safety Check Sheet

Yes   No   STEERING AND WHEEL ALIGNMENT

☐   ☐   Play in steering wheel does not exceed $1^1/_2$ to 3 inches.

☐   ☐   Car steers easily.

EXHAUST SYSTEM AND MUFFLER

☐   ☐   Tight—no carbon monoxide seepage into car through holes or leaks

☐   ☐   Quiet

WINDSHIELD WIPERS

☐   ☐   Dependable—work when needed

☐   ☐   Flexible rubber blades that wipe clean

☐   ☐   Run at an adequate and constant speed

GLASS

☐   ☐   Free from cracks, chips, discoloration, or dirt that obscures vision

☐   ☐   Free from unnecessary stickers and objects that obscure vision

☐   ☐   Clean and free of dirt or film

HORN

☐   ☐   Sounds off when properly depressed

☐   ☐   Loud enough to be heard 200 feet away but not so loud that it is a nuisance

☐   ☐   Operates from any part of horn assembly

OTHER

☐   ☐   Seat belts in good working order

☐   ☐   Flashlight in car

☐   ☐   No objects on back seat that obstruct vision

☐   ☐   Defroster works properly with good flow of air.

☐   ☐   Sun visors work freely, yet stay as positioned.

Adapted from "Unit 1: The Car and the Highway." 4-H Automotive Care and Safety Project.

Chapter 11 Health and Safety

Activity 11-8   Safety Practices Self-rating

Rate yourself on each of the following safety practices. **Always**   **Usually**   **Seldom**   **Never**

1. I pick up shoes, books, and other objects from stairs and floors. _______ _______ _______ _______

2. I put kitchen knives, other utensils, tools, and household cleaners away immediately after use. _______ _______ _______ _______

3. I use a ladder or firm chair to reach objects in high places. _______ _______ _______ _______

4. I turn pot handles toward the back of the range. _______ _______ _______ _______

5. I immediately wipe up water, grease, or anything else spilled on the floor. _______ _______ _______ _______

6. I dry my hands before using a hair dryer, razor, or other electrical appliance. _______ _______ _______ _______

7. I keep radios and similar electrical appliances out of the bathroom. _______ _______ _______ _______

8. I wear a shirt, pants, and heavy work shoes when using a lawn mower. _______ _______ _______ _______

9. I cooperate with teachers and other school officials in following safety instructions. _______ _______ _______ _______

10. I do not run, crowd, or shove in school halls or stairways. _______ _______ _______ _______

11. I do not throw pens, pencils, paper clips, or other objects in school. _______ _______ _______ _______

12. I learn and obey job safety rules and regulations.

13. I consult the job procedures manual or ask my supervisor or experienced coworkers about things I do not know how to do. _______ _______ _______ _______

14. I watch for safety hazards on the job.

15. I report job accidents and injuries. _______ _______ _______ _______

16. I try to set a good example for other workers regarding safety on the job. _______ _______ _______ _______

17. I perform as trained on the job. _______ _______ _______ _______

18. I use proper equipment and clothing in recreational activities. _______ _______ _______ _______

(Continued on next page)

Chapter 11 Health and Safety   109

Activity 11-8 Safety Practices Self-rating

	Always	Usually	Seldom	Never
19. I avoid overexertion in recreation.	______	______	______	______
20. I do not swim alone or take chances around water.	______	______	______	______
21. I observe motor vehicle speed limits.	______	______	______	______
22. I am a courteous driver.	______	______	______	______
23. I stay a safe distance behind other vehicles when driving.	______	______	______	______
24. I do not operate motor vehicles under the influence of drugs or alcohol.	______	______	______	______
25. I use a safety belt when operating a motor vehicle.	______	______	______	______

How safety-conscious are you? Review the ratings and give yourself an overall safety rating as follows:

________ Outstanding   ________ Good   ________ Average   ________ Weak

26. In what area of personal accident prevention are you most in need of improvement—home, school, job, recreation, or automobile?

____

Explain what you need to do to improve in this area.

____

____

____

____

____

____

____

                                          Chapter 11 Health and Safety

Activity 11-9   Safety Organizations

Think Critically 32 on page 283 of your text lists 14 government agencies and private organizations that work in the field of personal and public safety and asks you to research an organization and prepare a short, written report. Use this page and the next to assist you in gathering and organizing the information for your report.

Source

Author(s) ____

Title: ____

Date of publication: __________ Publisher: _________________________________

Place of publication (if on the Web, list the URL): ___________________________________

____ Pages: ______________

Notes

When the organization was founded: __________   The purpose of the organization __________

____

Types of activities in which it engages: ____

____

____

____

____

____

How it is supported:

____

____

____

____

(Continued on next page)

Activity 11-9   Safety Organizations

Other information: ____

____

____

____

____

____

____

Organization

Introduction: ____

____

Main point and supporting ideas: _______________________________

____

____

Main point and supporting ideas: _______________________________

____

____

Main point and supporting ideas: _______________________________

____

____

Conclusion: ____

____

____

     Chapter 11 Health and Safety

Chapter 12   Leadership and Business Ownership

12-1   Organizational Leadership

Activity 12-1   Leadership Characteristics
Objective: To recall characteristics associated with leadership

Activity 12-2   Career and Technical Student Organizations
Objective: To describe the purpose, activities, and benefits of membership in a specific career and technical student organization

12-2   Parliamentary Procedure

Activity 12-3   Parliamentary Terms and Procedures
Objective: To identify terms, concepts, and procedures associated with parliamentary procedure

12-3   Self-employment

Activity 12-4   Interviewing an Entrepreneur
Objective: To interview a small business owner

Activity 12-5   Advantages and Disadvantages of a Small Business
Objective: To identify and explain the advantages and disadvantages of being a small business owner

12-4   Small Business and You

Activity 12-6   Entrepreneur Rating Scale
Objective: To judge yourself in relation to traits considered important for success in business

Activity 12-7   Planning for a Small Business
Objective: To recommend steps to take and information to gather when planning for a small business

Activity 12-1   Leadership Characteristics

Circle the letter T for each true statement and the letter F for each false statement.

T   F   1. The terms "leadership" and "management" mean the same thing.

T   F   2. The leader's job is to set a direction for the group and to inspire and motivate.

T   F   3. The manager's job is to direct people and resources toward achieving goals.

T   F   4. In small organizations, one person may be both the leader and manager.

T   F   5. Authoritarian leaders make decisions after receiving group input.

T   F   6. "Bossy" and "dictatorial" often describes authoritarian leaders.

T   F   7. Participative leadership style is commonly known as democratic leadership.

T   F   8. Participative leaders are very autocratic.

T   F   9. The delegative leadership style is usually the most effective style.

T   F   10. Delegative leaders often provide little guidance or direction to the group.

T   F   11. The best leaders do most of the work themselves.

T   F   12. Leaders have a vision of where they want the organization to go.

T   F   13. Leaders are found in every type of public and private organization.

T   F   14. A leader is always the person in charge of a meeting or organization.

T   F   15. You can usually tell a leader by his or her appearance.

T   F   16. Leaders view information as something to be kept to themselves.

T   F   17. Not all leaders are naturally gifted communicators.

T   F   18. Leaders try to be good role models and an inspiration for employees.

T   F   19. A leader is usually the most intelligent and skilled person in the organization.

T   F   20. Effective leaders do what they say they are going to do.

T   F   21. Good leaders often have favorite employees they rely on and reward.

T   F   22. Most leaders are willing to accept an average level of performance.

T   F   23. Leaders are expected to be fair and objective.

T   F   24. Effective leaders show respect for employees and provide encouragement.

T   F   25. Successful leaders share common characteristics, but a given leader might not be strong in all characteristics.

    Chapter 12 Leadership and Business Ownership

Activity 12-2   Career and Technical Student Organizations

In Activity 2 on page 311 of your text, you found out the types of career and technical student organizations in your school. In which organization are you most interested? Write the name below and answer the following questions about the organization.

1. What is the purpose of the organization? ____________________________________

   ____

   ____

2. What are five activities conducted by the organization to promote leadership skills and

   good citizenship? ____

   ____

   ____

3. What support and opportunities are provided by the national organization?

   ____

   ____

4. How might you personally benefit by joining this organization?

   ____

   ____

   ____

Chapter 12 Leadership and Business Ownership

Activity 12-3　Parliamentary Terms and Procedures

Match the phrase in the right column with the correct term on the left.

________   1. Parliamentary procedure　　a.　The standard steps covered in a meeting

________   2. Bylaws　　b.　A written record of a meeting

________   3. Majority　　c.　These define the basic characteristics of an organization and describe how it will operate.

________   4. Quorum　　d.　Rank of priority

________   5. Order of business　　e.　Rules to conduct a meeting in a fair and orderly manner

________   6. Motion　　f.　A majority of the membership

________   7. Precedence　　g.　An authority on rules

________   8. Parliamentarian　　h.　Support (a motion)

________   9. Minutes　　i.　A brief statement of a proposed action

________   10. Second　　j.　One more than half of the voters

The steps involved in making, discussing, and disposing of a motion are listed below in scrambled order. Number the steps from 1 to 10 in their correct order.

________   1. Motion is discussed (debated).

________   2. Motion is stated.

________   3. Members vote on the motion.

________   4. Member obtains the floor by rising and addressing the chair.

________   5. Member moves for adjournment.

________   6. Chair recognizes the member.

________   7. Chair announces results of the vote.

________   8. Motion is seconded (usually).

________   9. Discussion ends after all who wish to have spoken.

________   10. Chair restates the motion.

Activity 12-4 Interviewing an Entrepreneur

Identify a small business owner in your community to interview. Interview the person and fill in answers to the following questions.

1. Person interviewed: ____

2. Name of business: ____

3. What goods are sold, or what services are provided? _______________________________

4. How many full-time employees do you have? ____________ Part-time employees? _______

   People employed on an occasional basis (e.g., attorney, bookkeeper)? ________________

   ____

5. What are the six most important job tasks that you perform?

   _____________________________   _____________________________

   _____________________________   _____________________________

   _____________________________   _____________________________

6. What type of educational background did you have before you started this business?

   ____

   ____

7. What type of work experience did you have before you started this business?

   ____

   ____

8. Which was more valuable, your educational background or your work experience?

   _____________________________ Why? _____________________________

   ____

   ____

   ____

   ____

(Continued on next page)

Activity 12-4   Interviewing an Entrepreneur

9. Have you taken any additional educational courses or training since opening the business?

If so, what kind? ____

____

____

10. How many hours do you work each week? _________

11. How much vacation time do you have each year? _________

12. What three things do you like most about your business?

____

____

____

13. What three things do you like least?

____

____

____

14. If you had it to do over again, would you do the same things? ________ Why or why not?

____

____

____

Use the additional space for your own questions and comments.

____

____

____

____

____

____

____

Activity 12-5   Advantages and Disadvantages of a Small Business

List as many advantages and disadvantages as you can (up to ten of each) of being a small business owner.

Advantages	Disadvantages
1. _________________________	_________________________
2. _________________________	_________________________
3. _________________________	_________________________
4. _________________________	_________________________
5. _________________________	_________________________
6. _________________________	_________________________
7. _________________________	_________________________
8. _________________________	_________________________
9. _________________________	_________________________
10. ________________________	_________________________

In your opinion, do the advantages outweigh the disadvantages? Explain your answer.

____

____

____

Some people who do not want to operate a full-time business find that a part-time or seasonal business meets their needs. List as many examples as you can of businesses that can be successfully conducted on a part-time or seasonal basis.

____

____

____

____

Chapter 12 Leadership and Business Ownership   119

Activity 12-6   Entrepreneur Rating Scale

To be successful in business, you must honestly evaluate your strengths and weaknesses. Rate each of the following traits by checking off the appropriate response.

ENTREPRENEUR RATING SCALE

	Yes	Not Sure	No
1. I am a self-starter. I get things done.			
2. I like people. I can get along with just about anybody			
3. I am a leader. I can get most people to go along when I start something.			
4. I like to take charge of things and see them through.			
5. I like to have a plan before I start. I'm usually the one to get things lined up when our group wants to do something.			
6. I like working hard for something I want.			
7. I can make up my mind in a hurry if I want to.			
8. People can trust me. I do what I say.			
9. If I make up my mind to do something, I'll see it through.			
10. I am always careful to write things down and to keep good records.			

Source: *Starting and Managing a Small Business of Your Own*, Small Business Administration.

How many **yes** answers did you circle? _________ Based on your responses, are you the type to run your own business? _________ Explain your answer. ___________________________________

____

____

____

If you are the type to run your own business, what type of business might you start? _______

____

____

____

Chapter 12 Leadership and Business Ownership

Activity 12-7   Planning for a Small Business

Enrique is a work experience student who works at a local hospital. He thinks that he might someday want to have his own business traveling to people's homes and doing medical exams for insurance companies of people applying for life insurance. He has assessed his strengths and weaknesses and believes that he has the personality to be an entrepreneur.

1. What is the best way for Enrique to learn about this business? ____________________

____

2. What are some basic skills (not medical skills) that Enrique should try to learn in school to prepare himself for this business?

____

____

____

3. List eight types of resources for Enrique to get facts about the business he wants to start.

4. Can you think of some ways that Enrique might find out if there are potential customers for his business? Describe two possible sources of information.

____

____

____

5. How can Enrique find out if this is a field in which growth is expected? Describe two possible sources of information.

____

____

____

Chapter 12 Leadership and Business Ownership   121

Chapter 13   Computer and Technology Skills

13-1   How Computers Work

Activity 13-1   Occupations and Computers
Objective: To describe how computers are used in relation to an occupation of interest

13-2   Computer Hardware and Software

Activity 13-2   Computer Literacy
Objective: To name terms and concepts associated with computer operation

Activity 13-3   Working with Spreadsheets
Objective: To explain numerical data with a spreadsheet, chart, and text

13-3   The Internet and Future of Computers

Activity 13-4   Finding Specific Web Information
Objective: To use various Web information sources

Activity 13-5   About the Web
Objective: To explain how the Web has evolved

Activity 13-1   Occupations and Computers

Which occupation are you currently preparing for or do you hope to follow upon completing

your education and training? ____

Investigate and then list as many ways as you can (up to ten) in which computers are being used in this occupation.

____   ____

____   ____

____   ____

____   ____

Describe a major occupational task now done by computers that could not be done, or could be

done only with great difficulty, without them. _______________________________________

____

____

____

____

____

____

How would you rate the need to understand and operate computers in relation to the occupation listed? (Circle one.)

Absolutely Essential	**Essential**	**Desirable**	**Little Need**	**No Need**

Activity 13-2   Computer Literacy

______ 1. Computer   a. Devices located outside the CPU

______ 2. Keyboard   b. Preprogrammed, permanent memory

______ 3. Graphic user interface (GUI)   c. A CPU on a single chip

______ 4. Program   d. Where data and programs are recorded and stored

______ 5. RAM   e. An operating system that provides icons and menus to click on

______ 6. ROM   f. Let users enter information and change it into electronic signals the computer can use

______ 7. Peripherals   g. Directs traffic within the computer

______ 8. Microprocessor   h. An electronic tool

______ 9. Monitor   i. The heart of the computer; does the actual processing

______ 10. Input devices   j. Used for manually inputting letters or numbers

______ 11. Memory   k. Transform electronic language into forms interpretable by humans

______ 12. Arithmetic and logic   l. Consists of instructions to a computer on how to solve a certain problem or do a certain task

______ 13. Control   m. Two or more computers linked together by cable or wireless means

______ 14. Output devices   n. Working memory

______ 15. Network   o. Output device for viewing data or graphics

Briefly explain the input–processing–output sequence of a computer.

____

____

____

____

   Chapter 13 Computer and Technology Skills

Activity 13-3   Working with Spreadsheets

Spreadsheets are not just useful for making calculations. They can be helpful in reports, presentations, or any time you need to present numerical data to others. Numbers arranged in rows and columns can be easier to understand than paragraphs of text. With the chart feature of spreadsheet software, you can create illustrations that can make the meaning of information even more clear.

1. Find some numerical data in a newspaper or magazine or on the Web. If you have access to the Web, a good resource is FedStats at *www.fedstats.gov/*.

2. Create a spreadsheet from your data.

3. Use the chart feature of your spreadsheet software to make a chart that illustrates the data. Print your spreadsheet and pie chart.

4. In the space below, write a paragraph that interprets or comments on your data.

Chapter 13 Computer and Technology Skills

Activity 13-4   Finding Specific Web Information

Following are a number of sources and strategies that will help you locate specific types of information. For each source, key in the URL that connects you to the website. Then, select a topic or type of information to research and summarize what you learned.

1. **SweetSearch2Day** is where you can learn something new each day. (*http://2day.sweetsearch.com/*)

____

____

____

____

2. **Times Topics** is used to find recent information along with analysis. (*www.nytimes.com/pages/topics/*)

____

____

____

____

3. **HeadlinesSpot** is a place to find opinions and newspaper editorials on current issues. (*www.headlinespot.com/type/newspapers*)

____

____

____

____

4. **American Memory** is used to locate primary (original) sources of documents, sound recordings, images, and maps from America's history. (*http://memory.loc.gov/ammem/browse/*)

____

____

____

____

5. **American Rhetoric** is a place to find speeches by famous persons. (*www.americanrhetoric.com*)

____

____

____

____

(Continued on next page)

                                    Chapter 13 Computer and Technology Skills

Activity 13-4   Finding Specific Web Information

6. **AmericanFactFinder** is used to find statistical information and data.
   (*http://factfinder2.census.gov/faces/nav/jsf/pages/index.xhtml*)

____

____

____

____

7. **Mayo Clinic** provides a reliable source for health information. (*www.mayoclinic.com*)

____

____

____

____

8. **Biography.com** is the place to find facts and information about people.
   (*www.biography.com/people/*)

____

____

____

____

9. **Legal Information Institute** is a source for information about legal issues.
   (*www.law.cornell.edu*)

____

____

____

10. **Maps** provides maps and other geographic information.
    (*http://maps.nationalgeographic.com/*)

____

____

____

Follow-up: For dozens of additional research tools to meet your specific information needs, go to *www.noodletools.com/* and click on "Choose the Best Search." Browse the site and try out additional resources. Also, click on "NoodleQuest" for an interactive version of this website. What other resources did you use?

____

____

Chapter 13 Computer and Technology Skills   127

Activity 13-5   About the Web

Review pages 326–331 in the textbook and search the Internet for information to answer the following questions.

1. The first web browser was invented in 1990. What was it called?

   ____

2. The first popular browser software was introduced in 1993. What was it called?

   ____

3. Currently, what are the four most popular Internet browsers?

   ____

4. Briefly summarize what is meant by Web 1.0 and provide examples to illustrate your answer.

   ____

   ____

   ____

   ____

5. How is Web 2.0 different from Web 1.0? Explain and provide examples of technologies that have led this revolution.

   ____

   ____

   ____

   ____

6. Some experts believe that the third decade (2010–2020) of Web development, called Web 3.0, is already underway. What is Web 3.0? Explain and provide examples to illustrate your answer.

   ____

   ____

   ____

   ____

                                    Chapter 13 Computer and Technology Skills

Chapter 14   The Economic World

14-1   Principles of Economics

Activity 14-1   Economic Growth
Objective: To understand concepts associated with economic growth

Activity 14-2   Circular Flow of Economic Activity
Objective: To explain and illustrate the circular flow of economic activity

14-2   The American Free Enterprise System

Activity 14-3   Economics Terminology
Objective: To name terms and concepts associated with economics

14-3   The Global Economy

Activity 14-4   Globalization
Objective: To explain how a selected country has been influenced by globalization

Activity 14-1   Economic Growth

1. The United States' abundant natural resources have contributed significantly to its economic growth. Suppose you governed a country that was poor in natural resources. How could you still achieve economic growth?

____

____

2. You have read that the four factors of production are used to produce capital goods and consumer goods and services. Which factor of production does every person possess?

____

3. You have read that capital goods are any person-made means of production, such as tools, machines, and factories. They are goods that can be used to produce other goods and services. Your school building is an example of a capital good. The building can be used over and over to educate people. The blackboard or whiteboard in your classroom is another example. List two more examples:

____

____

____

4. Capital goods make people more productive. Use an example to explain why this is so.

____

____

____

5. Where do businesses get the money to buy capital goods?

____

____

6. Suppose interest rates for borrowing money rise, as often happens in periods of inflation. What will happen to the demand for capital goods?

____

____

7. "The American dream" has to do with economic opportunity and material success. What is another example of how our society demonstrates that it is generally pro-work?

____

____

Activity 14-2   Circular Flow of Economic Activity

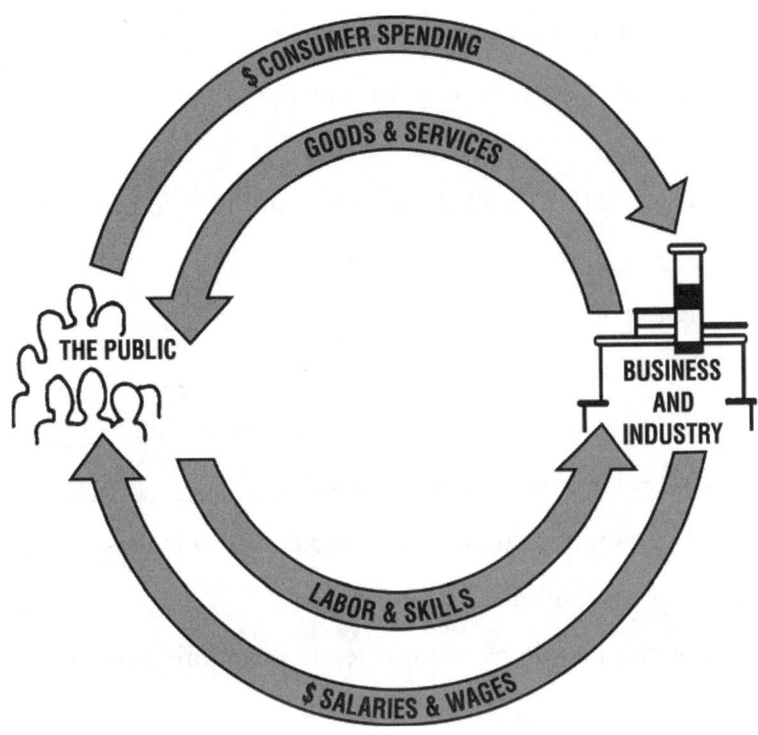

1. Provide a specific example to illustrate how the circular flow of economic activity shown actually works.

____

____

____

2. Place an X over one of the four half-cycle arrows shown, thereby interrupting the "circular flow." Then explain what influence this interruption has on the remaining three half-cycles.

____

____

____

____

____

____

____

____

Chapter 14 The Economic World

Activity 14-3   Economics Terminology

Fill in the correct word(s) in the spaces provided.

1. The study of how goods and services are produced, distributed, and used:

   _ _ _ _ _ _ _ _ _

2. Using natural resources, labor, capital, and management to provide goods and services:

   _ _ _ _ _ _ _ _ _ _

3. Any person-made means of production: _ _ _ _ _ _ _

4. The process of using goods and services: _ _ _ _ _ _ _ _ _ _ _

5. This is created whenever goods or services are bought or sold: _ _ _ _ _ _

6. The amount of goods or services available for sale: _ _ _ _ _ _

7. 7. The willingness of consumers to purchase goods and services: _ _ _ _ _ _

8. The efforts of sellers to win potential customers: _ _ _ _ _ _ _ _ _ _

9. Type of economy in which people have no voice in economic decision making:

   _ _ _ _ _ _ _ _ _   _ _ _ _ _ _ _

10. Type of economy in which individuals and businesses can do more or less as they please:

    _ _ _ _   _ _ _ _ _ _ _ _ _

11. An economy that has features of both items 9 and 10 above: _ _ _ _ _ _

12. The excess of income over expenditures: _ _ _ _ _ _

13. Exclusive control over the supply of a product or service: _ _ _ _ _ _ _ _

14. In a free enterprise economy, markets are: _ _ _ _ _-_ _ _ _ _ _ _ _ _

15. A period of expanding economic growth: _ _ _ _ _ _ _ _ _ _

16. A downturn in the economy: _ _ _ _ _ _ _ _ _

17. A severe contraction in the economy marked by stagnant business activity:

    _ _ _ _ _ _ _ _ _

18. A sharp increase in the prices of goods and services: _ _ _ _ _ _ _ _ _

19. How much has been spent over budget or over what has been taken in: _ _ _ _ _ _ _

20. A collection of rights that allow people to make free choices:

    _ _ _ _ _ _ _ _   _ _ _ _ _ _ _

   Chapter 14 The Economic World

Activity 14-4   Globalization

Review pages 352–354 in the textbook regarding the three major influences on globalization. Then, complete the following activity.

Select one of the following countries (India, China, Russia, South Korea, or Brazil) or

another country of interest. Name the country of interest: _________________________________

For the country selected, conduct research to answer the following four questions.

1. How have *changes in transportation* influenced the country?

____

____

____

____

2. How has *new communication technology* influenced the country?

____

____

____

____

3. How has *free enterprise* influenced the country?

____

____

____

____

4. Overall, has globalization had more of a positive or negative influence on the country?

____

____

____

____

Chapter 14 The Economic World   **133**

Chapter 15   The Consumer in the Marketplace

15-1   You as a Consumer

Activity 15-1   **Comparison Shopping**
Objective: To compare the costs of selected products at three different types of stores

15-2   Advertising and the Consumer

Activity 15-2   **Advertising Techniques**
Objective: To explain how a specific piece of advertising accomplishes four steps involved in selling

Activity 15-3   **Sales Come-ons**
Objective: To explain the message contained in various advertising statements

15-3   Consumer Rights and Responsibilities

Activity 15-4   **Letter of Complaint**
Objective: To write a hypothetical letter of complaint about a consumer problem

Activity 15-5   **Used Car Prices**
Objective: To obtain information about a used car from the *NADA Used Car Guide* or its website

Activity 15-1   Comparison Shopping

For each type of product listed, select a popular brand and size. Then go to each of the three types of stores indicated and record the selling price for the products.

	Brand	Size	Convenience Store	Grocery Store	Discount Store
1. Toothpaste	_________	_______	_________	_________	_________
2. Bath soap	_________	_______	_________	_________	_________
3. Deodorant	_________	_______	_________	_________	_________
4. Shampoo	_________	_______	_________	_________	_________
5. Pain reliever	_________	_______	_________	_________	_________
6. Antacid	_________	_______	_________	_________	_________
7. Cold remedy	_________	_______	_________	_________	_________
8. Juices	_________	_______	_________	_________	_________
9. Granola bars	_________	_______	_________	_________	_________
10. Dog food	_________	_______	_________	_________	_________
Total	_________	_______	$_________	$_________	$_________

Give several examples and prices of store brands or generic products that you could purchase instead of a national brand.

____

____

The grocery store probably has some products sold in bulk that you can package yourself. Give several examples of the cost of bulk products compared to prepackaged products.

____

____

Generally you can save money buying generic brands and bulk products. Can you think of instances, however, in which generic brands or bulk products may actually cost more?

____

____

Chapter 15 The Consumer in the Marketplace

Activity 15-2   Advertising Techniques

Selling can be divided into four steps, listed below. Cut an ad from an old magazine that illustrates the four steps. Attach the ad to this sheet. Explain how the ad accomplishes each step.

1. Attracting the buyer's attention: ____

____

____

____

____

2. Getting the buyer interested: ____

____

____

____

____

____

3. Creating a desire to buy: ____

____

____

____

____

4. Encouraging the buyer to take action: ____

____

____

____

____

   Chapter 15 The Consumer in the Marketplace

Activity 15-3   Sales Come-ons

Even the most reputable store may exaggerate in its advertisements from time to time. What does each of these statements from ads really tell you or not tell you?

1. "Up to 50 percent off" ____

____

____

2. "Our lowest prices ever!" ____

____

____

3. "Storewide sale on selected items" _______________________________________

____

____

4. "Tremendous savings while quantities last!" ______________________________

____

____

5. "Sold elsewhere for . . ." ____

____

____

6. "Ridiculous, giveaway prices" ____

____

____

7. "Items shown typical of merchandise available" ___________________________

____

____

8. "Huge truckload sale" ____

____

____

Activity 15-4   Letter of Complaint

Assume that on May 15, 20__, you purchased a Total Sound car audio system with a 12-month warranty from Hank's Stereo in Phoenix, AZ. The CD player quit working on May 22 of the following year, one week after the warranty expired. It is defective, but the dealer will not fix it because the warranty has expired. Write a letter of complaint to the manufacturer (Total Sound, Inc., 1403 Broad St., Lansing, MI 48901-3475). Use the return address 15 Echo Ave., Phoenix, AZ 85001-4493. The serial number of the player is 87492. Date the letter May 25.

                                    Chapter 15 The Consumer in the Marketplace

Activity 15-5   Used Car Prices

Name a three- to five-year-old automobile and model that you would like to own (be realistic):

____

Obtain a recent copy of the *NADA Used Car Guide* at a library or on the Web (*www.nadaguides.com*). Locate information for the auto listed and answer the following questions.

1. What is the average retail price for the car? ____

2. List three to five options for the car. How much would each add to the average retail price?

____

____

____

____

3. What would be the total retail price of the auto with all of the options added? _____________

4. Locate the mileage tables. How much would you add to the cost if your chosen car had

   20,000 miles less than the Trade-In value? ____

   How much would you deduct from the cost if your chosen car had 20,000 miles more than

   the Trade-In? ____

   ____

5. If you were trading in a car like the one listed, what would be its average trade-in value?

   ____

6. How can resources such as the NADA, Kelley Blue Book, or Edmunds websites or print

   publications help you when shopping for a used car? ____

   ____

   ____

7. What other important factors, in addition to average listed price, should you consider in

   deciding how much to pay for a used car? ____

   ____

   ____

Chapter 15 The Consumer in the Marketplace   139

Chapter 16 Banking and Credit

16-1 Financial Institutions

Activity 16-1 **Financial Institutions**
Objective: To recall characteristics associated with financial institutions and the banking system

16-2 Checking Accounts

Activity 16-2 **Managing a Checking Account**
Objective: To write and endorse a check, complete a deposit ticket, and record information in a check register

Activity 16-3 **Balancing a Bank Statement**
Objective: To balance an account statement

16-3 Credit and Its Use

Activity 16-4 **The Cost of Credit**
Objective: To complete various questions and problems regarding the cost of credit

Activity 16-5 **Credit Application**
Objective: To practice filling out a credit application

Activity 16-1 Financial Institutions

Circle the letter T for each true statement and the letter F for each false statement.

T F 1. Mutual savings banks are the most common type of financial institution.

T F 2. Commercial banks are often described as "full-service" banks.

T F 3. Mutual savings banks tend to pay a lower rate of interest than commercial banks.

T F 4. Savings and loan associations are the only type of bank to offer mortgage financing.

T F 5. A mutual savings bank is owned by its depositors.

T F 6. Credit unions are insured by the FDIC.

T F 7. Savings and loan associations were created to provide financing for home construction.

T F 8. Credit unions are nonprofit savings and loan cooperative associations.

T F 9. The four major types of financial institutions offer vastly different services.

T F 10. Any annual profit earned by a credit union is distributed to its members.

T F 11. Most common banking transactions can be done online.

T F 12. Unlike a credit card, a debit card transaction is immediately transferred from your account.

T F 13. The 2008 economic crisis had little relationship to the housing market.

T F 14. The median price of an American home has increased steadily from the mid-1940s to the present.

T F 15. A "housing bubble" refers to the run-up in housing prices fueled by demand and speculation.

T F 16. "Flipping" a home refers to the practice of purchasing a home or condominium with the intent of reselling it for a profit.

T F 17. Working with a predatory lender is a good choice for people seeking home mortgages.

T F 18. Leading up to 2006, many people bought homes that they could not afford.

T F 19. Despite the bursting housing bubble in 2006, home prices continued to increase.

T F 20. In October 2008, the U.S. financial system was on the verge of collapse.

T F 21. The majority of financial institutions in the U.S. are stable and well managed.

T F 22. Financial institutions in the United States are regulated by the Federal Reserve System.

T F 23. Deposits in a bank or credit union are insured up to $100,000 per account.

T F 24 When a bank fails and is taken over by the FDIC, customer accounts are quickly frozen.

T F 25. Studies have shown that more than 80% of customers are satisfied with their banking institution.

Chapter 16 Banking and Credit

141

Activity 16-2 Managing a Checking Account

Writing a Check

Fill out the check below for $47.16 to Chuck's Auto Service for repairs to your car. Use the date of April 8.

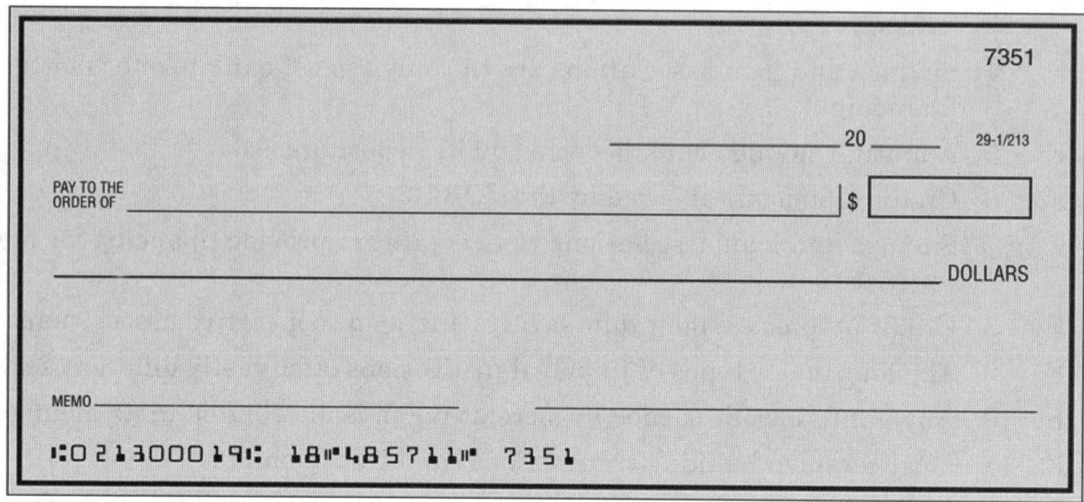

Endorsing a Check

Provide an example below of the three different forms of endorsement.

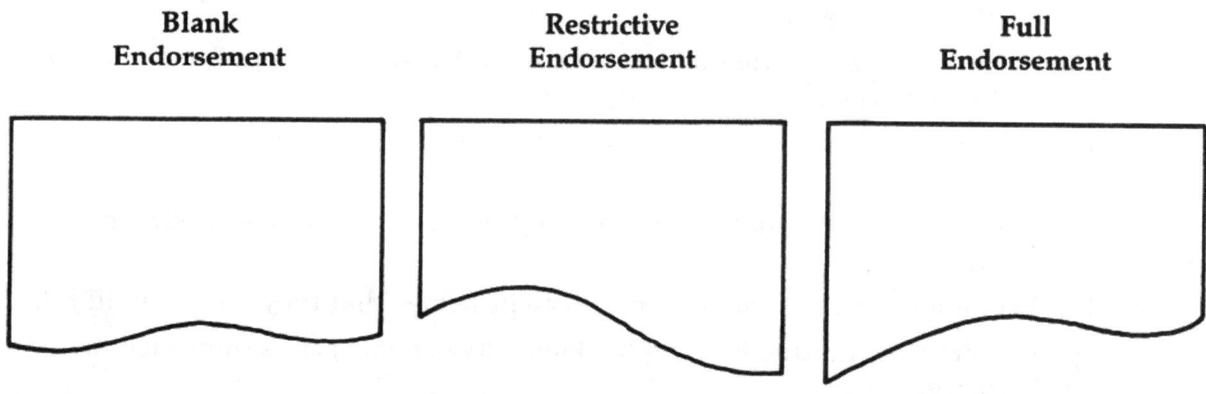

(Continued on next page)

          Chapter 16 Banking and Credit

Activity 16-2 Managing a Checking Account

Making a Deposit

You want to deposit $89.75 in cash, as well as checks in the amounts of $23.18 and $37.85.
Fill out the deposit ticket below using this information and the date of April 9.

DEPOSIT TICKET		CASH——▶		
		LIST CHECKS SINGLY.		
				29-1/213
____________ 20 __		TOTAL FROM OTHER SIDE		USE OTHER SIDE FOR ADDITIONAL LISTINGS. ◀ENTER TOTAL HERE.
		TOTAL ITEMS	TOTAL	BE SURE EACH ITEM IS PROPERLY ENDORSED.

⑆0 2 ‖3000‖9⑆ ‖8⑈48 5 7 ‖‖⑈

CHECKS AND OTHER ITEMS ARE RECEIVED FOR DEPOSIT SUBJECT TO THE PROVISIONS OF THE UNIFORM COMMERCIAL CODE OR ANY APPLICABLE COLLECTION AGREEMENT.

Keeping a Checkbook Register

You have a checkbook balance of $235.46. Record the check you wrote to Chuck's Auto
Service and the deposit you just made. Assume that you wrote two additional checks on April
10, to Record Mart for $12.37 and to Kavnar's Grocery for $31.53. Enter this information in
the register below.

		RECORD ALL CHARGES OR CREDITS THAT AFFECT YOUR ACCOUNT.					BALANCE	
NUMBER	DATE	DESCRIPTION OF TRANSACTION	PAYMENT/DEBIT (-)	✓ T	FEE (IF ANY) (-)	DEPOSIT/CREDIT (+)	$	
			$		$	$		

Activity 16-3 Balancing a Bank Statement

Use the following information to balance your bank statement. The balance on the form should equal the balance in your checkbook register.

Statement balance: $437.62 **Checkbook balance:** $371.90 **Interest paid:** $1.82
Outstanding checks: **Deposits not credited:** **Service charge:** $5.00
#273, $103.22 $37.46
#276, $14.34 $18.91
#277, $7.71

MONTH _______________________________ 20 __________

THIS FORM IS PROVIDED TO HELP YOU BALANCE YOUR ACCOUNT STATEMENT.

**CHECKS OUTSTANDING
NOT CHARGED TO YOUR ACCOUNT**

NO	$	
TOTAL	$	

ENDING BALANCE SHOWN ON THIS STATEMENT $__________

ADD ANY DEPOSITS NOT CREDITED IN THIS STATEMENT   __________

TOTAL $ __________

→ SUBTRACT ANY CHECKS OUTSTANDING   __________

BALANCE $ __________ ←

CURRENT CHECKBOOK BALANCE $ __________

ADD ANY INTEREST PAYMENTS SHOWN ON THIS STATEMENT   __________

TOTAL $ __________

SUBTRACT ANY SERVICE OR OTHER CHARGES SHOWN ON THIS STATEMENT   __________

NEW CHECKBOOK BALANCE
should agree with $ __________

NOTE: Be certain to add to your register any interest paid and subtract from your register any miscellaneous charges (service charge, check printing charge, NSF charge, etc.) applied in the current statement period.

    Chapter 16 Banking and Credit

Activity 16-4 The Cost of Credit

Answer the following questions related to the cost of credit.

1. The total dollar amount you pay for using credit is the _______________________________

2. What types of charges may be included in the cost of using credit? _______________________

____

3. If you borrowed $2,000 for two years and paid $396 in interest, $12 for insurance, and a

   $5 service charge, how much was the finance charge you paid? _______________________

   What were your monthly payments? ____________

4. If you borrowed $1,600 for a year and paid interest of $106, what was the total cost of

   the loan? ____________ How much was the monthly payment? ____________

   How much interest was paid each month? ____________

5. The percentage cost of credit on a yearly basis is the ._______________________________

6. Explain why the APR for a loan paid back in monthly installments is higher than the

   APR for a loan paid back in one lump sum. _______________________________________

   ____

Assume that you are going to borrow $5,000 and that the following three options are available.
Look over these data and answer the following questions.

	APR	Length of Loan	Monthly Payment	Finance Charge	Total Cost
Creditor A	11%	36 months	$164	$893	$5,893
Creditor B	11%	48 months	$129	$1,203	$6,203
Creditor C	12%	48 months	$132	$1,320	$6,320

7. How much is the lowest possible monthly payment? ____________

8. If you chose Creditor A instead of Creditor B, how much would you save on finance

   charges? ____________

9. Suppose you are thinking of borrowing from Creditor C because it is offering a $50 gift

   certificate to new borrowers and the monthly payment is not much more than

   Creditor B's. Is this a good idea? Explain. _______________________________________

   ____

10. The cheapest credit is not to borrow money. List at least three things you should ask

    yourself before you borrow money or use sales credit. _______________________________

    ____

Chapter 16 Banking and Credit

Activity 16-5 Credit Application

Complete the following sample credit application form.

APPLICATION AND CHARGE AGREEMENT

Please complete all sections for faster processing. Please print.

Personal Information

Name (First, Middle, Last)	Social Security No.
Address (Street, City, State, ZIP)	Home Phone (With Area Code)

Age	Driver's License No.	No. of Dependent Children	How Long at Address ___Yrs. ___Mos.	☐ Own ☐ Live with Parents ☐ Rent

Previous Address (Street, City, State, ZIP)	How Long at Previous Address ___ Yrs. ___Mos.
Name (First, Middle Initial, Last) of Nearest Relative Not Living With You	Relative's Phone Number (With Area Code)
Relative's Address (Street, City, State, ZIP)	

Employment and Income

Employer	Type of Business
Business Address (Street, City, State, ZIP)	Position

Business Phone (With Area Code)	Monthly Salary	Length of Employment ___Yrs. ___Mos.

Name of Previous Employer (if Above Less Than One Year)	Type of Business
Business Address (Street, City, State, ZIP)	Position
Other Income Source (Optional). Alimony, child support, or separate maintenance income need not be revealed if you do not wish to have it considered as a basis for repaying this obligation.	Monthly Amount

Note: An applicant though married may apply for a separate account in his or her own name.

So your rights may be fully recognized, please indicate by a check mark if the following apply:	☐ My spouse will also use this account.	☐ My spouse's income should be considered in evaluating this application

Spouse's Name (First, Middle, Last)	
Spouse's Employer	Type of Business
Business Address (Street, City, State, ZIP)	Spouse's Position

Business Phone (With Area Code) :	Monthly Salary	Length of Employment ___Yrs. ___Mos.

Banking Facilities

Name of Facility (Checking)	Address (City, State)	Account No.
Name of Facility (Savings)	Address (City, State)	Account No.
Name of Facility (Loan)	Address (City, State)	Account No.

Credit References (if under a name other than Applicant's, please indicate)

Creditor	Address (City, State)	Account No.
Creditor	Address (City, State)	Account No.

Chapter 16 Banking and Credit

Chapter 17 Budget, Save, and Invest Money

17-1 Budget Money

Activity 17-1 **Record of Income and Expenditures**
Objective: To maintain a record of your income and expenditures

Activity 17-2 **Setting Financial Goals**
Objective: To identify and evaluate your future financial goals

Activity 17-3 **Preparing a Budget**
Objective: To develop a sample budget

17-2 Save Money

Activity 17-4 **Selecting a Savings Account**
Objective: To collect and evaluate information regarding savings account options

Activity 17-5 **Managing a Savings Account**
Objective: To fill out savings account deposit and withdrawal tickets

17-3 Invest Money

Activity 17-6 **Return on Savings and Investments**
Objective: To calculate the return on various forms of savings and investments

Activity 17-1   Record of Income

Use this form to keep a detailed record of all income and expenditures for one week.

RECORD OF INCOME AND EXPENDITURES

Week _______________________ 20 _______

Cash on hand _______________________

Date	Item	Income	

(Continued on next page)

Chapter 17 Budget, Save, and Invest Money

Activity 17-1   Record of Income

At the end of the week, study the records. List at least three things you notice about your spending.

1. ____

2. ____

3. ____

Summarize what you have learned about the pattern of your income and expenditures.

____

____

____

____

____

____

____

____

____

____

____

Activity 17-2   Setting Financial Goals

Write down your personal financial goals for the next year and the next five years.

Goals for this year: ____

____

____

____

Goals for the next five years: ____

____

____

____

How much monthly income do you think you will need to be able to achieve your five-year

goals? ____________________

Will your present educational and occupational plans result in your having the income to
achieve your financial goals? Explain:

____

____

____

____

One of the best ways to ensure that you will be able to achieve your financial goals is to invest
in a good education. Do your five-year goals include saving money for your education? Explain:

____

____

____

____

____

                                    Chapter 17 Budget, Save, and Invest Money

Activity 17-3   Preparing a Budget

Assume that you are married with one child and have a net monthly income of $___________.
Develop an estimated monthly budget using the following form.

<table>
<tr><td colspan="4" align="center">HOUSEHOLD BUDGET FORM</td></tr>
<tr><td colspan="4">Month ____________ 20 ____ Estimated Income _______________________________</td></tr>
<tr><td>Expenditure</td><td align="center">Estimate</td><td align="center">Actual</td><td align="center">Difference (+ or -)</td></tr>
<tr><td>Savings</td><td></td><td></td><td></td></tr>
<tr><td>Emergency reserve</td><td></td><td></td><td></td></tr>
<tr><td>Goals</td><td></td><td></td><td></td></tr>
<tr><td>Regular Expenses</td><td></td><td></td><td></td></tr>
<tr><td>Rent or mortgage payment</td><td></td><td></td><td></td></tr>
<tr><td>Utilities</td><td></td><td></td><td></td></tr>
<tr><td>Insurance</td><td></td><td></td><td></td></tr>
<tr><td>Auto payment</td><td></td><td></td><td></td></tr>
<tr><td>Credit or loan payments</td><td></td><td></td><td></td></tr>
<tr><td>Other ( )</td><td></td><td></td><td></td></tr>
<tr><td>Variable Expenses</td><td></td><td></td><td></td></tr>
<tr><td>Food and beverages</td><td></td><td></td><td></td></tr>
<tr><td>Clothing</td><td></td><td></td><td></td></tr>
<tr><td>Transportation</td><td></td><td></td><td></td></tr>
<tr><td>Household</td><td></td><td></td><td></td></tr>
<tr><td>Medical care</td><td></td><td></td><td></td></tr>
<tr><td>Entertainment</td><td></td><td></td><td></td></tr>
<tr><td>Gifts and contributions</td><td></td><td></td><td></td></tr>
<tr><td>Taxes</td><td></td><td></td><td></td></tr>
<tr><td>Other ( )</td><td></td><td></td><td></td></tr>
<tr><td>TOTALS</td><td></td><td></td><td></td></tr>
</table>

Activity 17-4   Selecting a Savings Account

Obtain information regarding passbook accounts from three different financial institutions in your area. Compare the institutions with respect to the following:

	Institution 1	Institution 2	Institution 3
1. What is the current interest rate?	_________	_________	_________
2. How often is the interest compounded?	_________	_________	_________
3. When is the interest paid?	_________	_________	_________
4. What is the APY?	_________	_________	_________
5. What is the minimum deposit?	_________	_________	_________

6. Describe any relevant service charges, rules, and restrictions.

Institution 1: ____

____

____

Institution 2: ____

____

____

Institution 3: ____

____

____

7. Based on the data you have collected, which of the three institutions has the best passbook

savings account? ____

8. In addition to cost factors, what other factors should you consider before opening a savings

account? ____

____

____

____

                    Chapter 17 Budget, Save, and Invest Money

Activity 17-5   Managing a Savings Account

Savings Deposit

You want to deposit $44.50 in cash and a check for $56.85 in a savings account (#4638-01). Fill out the deposit ticket below using this information and today's date.

SAVINGS DEPOSIT   DATE _________________

▶ ACCOUNT NUMBER ◯

	DOLLARS	CENTS
CASH		
LIST CHECKS SEPARATELY. BE SURE EACH ITEM IS ENDORSED.		
TOTAL DEPOSIT		

NAME _________________________________

TELLER'S STAMP

SUPERVISOR _________________________________

All unpaid items will be charged back to the depositor.

C - 153 500M 2/89-T

Savings Withdrawal

You want to withdraw $75.00 from a savings account (#4638-01). Fill out the following withdrawal ticket using this information and today's date.

SAVINGS WITHDRAWAL   DATE _________________

PAY TO _________________________________ **Or Bearer**

_________________________________ **Dollars**

I HEREBY CERTIFY ALL PERSONS NAMED IN THIS ACCOUNT ARE STILL LIVING.

ACCOUNT NUMBER ◯   ☐ CASH   ☐ CHECK   AMOUNT WITHDRAWN

TELLER'S STAMP

CHECK NUMBER _________________

____
SIGNATURE

____
SIGNATURE

SUPERVISOR _________________________________

C - 153 500M 2/89-T

PASSBOOK MUST ACCOMPANY THIS ORDER.

Chapter 17 Budget, Save, and Invest Money   153

Activity 17-6   Return on Savings and Investments

Answer the following questions related to the return on various forms of savings and investments.

1. What would be the return on a $1,200 savings account paying an APY of 8.5%? _________

2. You have a $2,000 certificate of deposit at a bank paying a 9% APY. How much money will you have at the end of 2 years, assuming that the interest is compounded annually? _____________

3. How much interest would you earn in a year on a $500 savings account paying 6% interest, compounded quarterly? __________ What would be the APY? ___________

4. How much interest would you earn in a year on a $3,000 savings account paying 7.5% interest, compounded semiannually? __________ What would be the APY? ___________

5. You bought 100 shares of stock selling at $18.50 a share and paid a commission of $35. What was the total cost of the stock purchase? ___________

6. You bought 100 shares of a company's stock for $32 a share. The company paid a quarterly dividend of $.48 a share. What was your annual dividend? ____________ What was the rate of return, assuming the stock price stayed the same? ____________________________

7. A stock that you bought at $27 a share increased in value to $42 a share. If you sold the stock, what would be your capital gain? ____

8. You bought 200 shares of stock for $25 a share and paying a $.20 quarterly dividend. You kept the stock for 2 years and sold it at $30 a share. Leaving out commissions, how much money did you earn? ____________ What was your annual rate of return? ____________

9. You bought a corporate bond for $1,000 that pays 7% interest quarterly. How much interest will you earn during the first quarter? ___________

10. A $1,000 corporate bond may be sold for more or less than the issue price. If you bought a $1,000 issue paying 6.5% for $950, what would be your actual rate of return? __________

   Chapter 17 Budget, Save, and Invest Money

Chapter 18   Insure Against Loss

18-1   Health Insurance

Activity 18-1   Nature of Insurance
Objective: To identify types of insurance risks and explain the basic nature of insurance

18-2   Life and Home Insurance

Activity 18-2   Insurance Protection
Objective: To name the term or concept associated with various types and characteristics of insurance

Activity 18-3   Renter's Insurance
Objective: To identify the need for renter's insurance and prepare a personal property inventory

18-3   Auto Insurance

Activity 18-4   Which Type of Insurance?
Objective: To identify the specific type of insurance coverage applicable in various situations

Activity 18-5   Automobile Insurance
Objective: To investigate and describe auto insurance laws in your state

Activity 18-1   Nature of Insurance

Match the type of insurance risk with various types of catastrophes.

a. Personal risks

b. Property risks

c. Liability risks

_____ 1. A major kitchen fire occurs in your home.

_____ 2. A family pet bites a child in your home.

_____ 3. You lose your job.

_____ 4. You have an auto accident.

_____ 5. You accidently cut yourself while slicing vegetables.

_____ 6. A child breaks the neighbor's window while playing baseball.

_____ 7. You have an illness that requires hospitalization.

_____ 8. Someone breaks into your home and steals electronic equipment.

_____ 9. A guest in your home slips getting into the bathtub.

_____ 10. You fall off a ladder and break several bones.

_____ 11. A person is injured in an auto accident that you caused.

_____ 12. A tornado destroys your home.

Answer the following questions regarding the nature of insurance.

13. Explain the basic idea that underlies all types of commercial insurance. _______________

____

____

____

____

14. If an uninsured person goes to an emergency room for medical care, who pays for the

medical services? ____

____

____

15. Do you think everyone should be mandated (required) to purchase health insurance
coverage? Answer and explain the basis for your position. ____________________

____

____

____

____

                                                    Chapter 18 Insure Against Loss

Activity 18-2 Insurance Protection

Complete the following word puzzle by filling in the correct term:

1. What people try to protect themselves against with insurance
2. A feature of major medical coverage that requires policyholders to share in the expenses
3. One of the three kinds of risks that people seek protection against
4. An amount that must be paid by a policyholder on a loss before the insurance company pays the balance
5. Insurance plans that usually provide more coverage and are less expensive than individual plans
6. A type of insurance that pays benefits to an individual who is out of work because of illness or injury
7. Costs resulting from illness or accident

(Continued on next page)

Activity 18-2   Insurance Protection

8. Person to whom insurance death benefits are paid

9. Regarding life insurance, the amount of money that is paid in the event of the insured's death (two words)

10. Something you should do with costs and coverages before you buy any type of insurance

11. Various types of damages for which you purchase home insurance

12. An alternative to traditional health insurance that covers preventative health care

13. A major, unexpected loss

14. The price of an insurance policy

15. A document that describes the terms of insurance coverage

16. Life insurance bought for a specified period of time

17. Another of the three kinds of risks that people seek protection against

18. The third of the three kinds of risks that people seek protection against

19. Another name for cash-value insurance

     Chapter 18 Insure Against Loss

Activity 18-3   Renter's Insurance

For whom is renter's insurance intended? ____

____

____

Assume that you and several of your friends plan to move into a furnished apartment in the near future. Complete an inventory of your personal property along with its estimated value. You may wish to group similar items together, such as clothes, jewelry, sporting equipment, and so on.

Item	Estimated Value
_________________________________	_________________
_________________________________	_________________
_________________________________	_________________
_________________________________	_________________
_________________________________	_________________
_________________________________	_________________
_________________________________	_________________
_________________________________	_________________
_________________________________	_________________
_________________________________	_________________

_________________________________ **Total**: $ _________________

What would be the approximate annual premium for a policy covering this amount of property?

(Allow an extra amount for things you will need to purchase.) ________________________

Why is it a good idea to photograph or videotape your personal property and to compile a

detailed inventory of it? ____

____

____

Chapter 18 Insure Against Loss   159

Activity 18-4   Which Type of Insurance?

All of the following individuals have insurance coverage. Indicate which specific type of insurance applies in each case.

1. Emilio had surgery to remove a ruptured appendix.

2. Catherine's expenses were for hospital care, laboratory fees, and medications.

3. Gus had a very serious heart condition that kept him in the hospital for several months. His expenses were more than $20,000.

4. Paul was charged $450 by his doctor for medical visits while he was in the hospital.

5. Virginia's insurance pays for regular office visits and checkups.

6. Steve was ill and missed six months' work. His insurance, however, provided a portion of his normal wages.

7. Minnie has money withheld from her paycheck each week for group life insurance. She has a five-year renewable policy.

8. Daryl makes semiannual payments on a $50,000 life insurance policy. He receives annual dividends and is able to borrow money against the policy.

9. Tom will pay the same annual premium on his life insurance policy until he reaches age 55, at which time it will be paid up.

10. Diana and Tony have insurance that covers their house and its contents.

11. Janet lives in an apartment and has her personal property insured.

12. Arthur's car was damaged by a hit-and-run driver.

13. The hood of Helen's car was dented by a wayward golf ball.

14. Joji drove into the back of another car, injuring the driver of the other vehicle.

15. While backing out of the driveway, Beverly ran over her neighbor's new bicycle.

16. Alex bumped Carolyn's fender at the parking garage. The repair costs were paid by each person's insurance company.

17. Eloisa and her daughter ran off the road and hit a tree. Both required hospital treatment.

18. Scott was driving home when his car slid into a bridge. He had to pay a $250 deductible for repairs.

Chapter 18 Insure Against Loss

Activity 18-5   Automobile Insurance

1. Briefly summarize the financial responsibility law in your state: _____________________

____

____

2. What is the penalty in your state for violation of the financial responsibility law? _______

____

____

3. Does your state have a law requiring automobile owners to have liability insurance? If so,

   describe the requirements: ____

____

____

4. Does your state have no-fault automobile insurance? If so, describe how it works: _______

____

____

5. Below is a listing of the six types of automobile insurance coverage. For each type, answer *yes* or *no* regarding whether the coverage applies to the policyholder and/or to other persons.

	Whom the Coverage Applies to:	
	Policyholder	**Other Persons**
a. Bodily injury liability	_____________	_____________
b. Property damage liability	_____________	_____________
c. Protection against uninsured motorists	_____________	_____________
d. Medical payments	_____________	_____________
e. Collision	_____________	_____________
f. Comprehensive	_____________	_____________

6. If you have an old car that is not worth much, which of the above types of coverage might

   you do without? ____

____

____

Chapter 19   Taxes, Taxation, and Retirement Planning

19-1   Taxation

Activity 19-1   Tax Rates
Objective: To illustrate differences between a graduated tax and a flat tax

19-2   File an Income Tax Return

Activity 19-2   Tax Terminology
Objective: To name the term or concept associated with taxes and taxation

Activity 19-3   Tax Rules
Objective: To explain the purpose served by various income tax rules

Activity 19-4   Filing a Tax Return
Objective: To complete a sample Form 1040EZ tax return

19-3   Social Security

Activity 19-5   Social Security Coverage
Objective: To recall facts and characteristics regarding social security coverage

Activity 19-6   Administration and Financing of Social Security
Objective: To answer questions and solve problems regarding the two types of social security programs

19-4   Individual Retirement Accounts

Activity 19-7   Individual Retirement Accounts
Objective: To calculate the tax savings resulting from an IRA

Activity 19-1   Tax Rates

The following table illustrates the relationship between a graduated tax and a flat tax.

TYPES OF TAXES				
	Graduated		Flat	
Income	Tax Rate	Tax	Tax Rate	Tax
$1,000	0	0	2%	$20
$2,000	0	0	2%	$40
$5,000	6.28%	$314	2%	$100
$7,000	8.51%	$596	2%	$140
$10,000	10.58%	$1,058	2%	$200
$20,000	15.65%	$3,130	2%	$400
$30,000	19.86%	$5,958	2%	$600
$40,000	23.84%	$9,536	2%	$800
$50,000	27.17%	$13,589	2%	$1,000

1. Answer these questions regarding a graduated tax.

   a. If your income was $2,000, how much tax would you owe? _______________________

   b. What is the tax rate for a person who earned $7,000? _______________________

   c. How much tax does a person who earned $20,000 have to pay? _______________________

   d. If your income increases three times, from $10,000 to $30,000, by how many times

   does your tax increase? _______________________________________

2. Answer these questions regarding a flat tax.

   a. If your income was $2,000, how much tax would you owe? _______________________

   b. What is the tax rate for a person who earned $7,000? _______________________

   c. How much tax does a person who earned $20,000 have to pay? _______________________

   d. If your income increases three times, from $10,000 to $30,000, by how many times

   does your tax increase? _______________________________________

3. What is the basic idea underlying a graduated tax? _______________________

   ____

4. What do you think is the basic idea underlying a flat tax? _______________________

   ____

5. Which type of tax do you think is fairer? Why? _______________________

   ____

Chapter 19 Taxes, Taxation, and Retirement Planning

Activity 19-2   Tax Terminology

Fill in the correct word(s) in the spaces provided.

1. The process by which the expenses of government are paid: __ __ __ __ __ __ __ __ __

2. A compulsory contribution of money made to government: __ __ __ __

3. Money that is raised through taxes to pay the cost of government: __ __ __ __ __ __ __ __

4. A tax that goes straight to the government: __ __ __ __ __ __ __

5. The tax you pay on money you earn: __ __ __ __ __ __ __

6. A tax that you and your employer pay to support Social Security: __ __ __ __ __ __ __ __

7. A tax that you pay on the amount of a purchase: __ __ __ __ __ __

8. A type of tax commonly paid on such items as gasoline, tires, and amusements:

   __ __ __ __ __ __

9. A tax assessed on a dead person's wealth and property: __ __ __ __ __ __

10. If someone leaves you money in a will, you may have to pay this tax:

    __ __ __ __ __ __ __ __ __ __

11. A tax paid on money or property given to you: __ __ __ __ __

12. A tax that increases in proportion to one's income: __ __ __ __ __ __ __ __ __ __

13. A tax for which the same rate applies regardless of income: __ __ __ __ __

14. Items such as alimony payments and individual retirement account contributions that

    may be deducted from your gross income: __ __ __ __ __ __ __ __ __ __ __ __ __

    __ __ __ __ __ __

15. After subtracting the items in 14 above from your income, you are left with an:

    __ __ __ __ __ __ __ __ __ __ __ __ __ __ __ __ __ __ __ __

16. Items such as mortgage interest and property taxes that you are allowed to subtract from

    adjusted gross income: __ __ __ __ __ __ __ __ __ __

17. Set amounts for yourself and each dependent that you can subtract:

    __ __ __ __ __ __ __ __ __ __

18. The amount of income on which you pay tax: __ __ __ __ __ __ __ __ __ __ __ __ __ __

19. Reductions in the amount of income tax owed for child care and other expenses:

    __ __ __ __ __ __ __ __ __ __

20. The crime of intentionally trying to avoid paying income taxes:

    __ __ __ __ __ __ __ __ __ __

21. The process of completing and submitting an income tax return: __ __ __ __ __ __

    Chapter 19 Taxes, Taxation, and Retirement Planning

Activity 19-3   Tax Rules

Many kinds of exemptions, deductions, and credits have been written into the tax law by Congress to accomplish certain purposes. Explain the purpose that you know or think might be served by the rules described in Items 1–7. Then answer Question 8.

1. Taxpayers who have children pay less tax. ____

____

2. An unmarried head of household pays less in tax than a single person. _______________

____

____

3. Interest on a home mortgage is tax-deductible. ___________________________________

____

____

4. Taxpayers may deduct money contributed to charity _______________________________

____

____

5. Almost every working person is eligible to make contributions to an individual retirement

account that can be deducted from his or her income tax. ___________________________

____

____

6. A tax credit can be taken for child-care expenses. ________________________________

____

____

7. You can deduct the cost of education required to keep your job and improve or maintain

your skills. ____

____

8. A number of wealthy people and corporations are able to avoid paying taxes. What is your

opinion of this? ____

____

Chapter 19 Taxes, Taxation, and Retirement Planning   **165**

Activity 19-4   Filing a Tax Return

Complete Form 1040EZ on the next page using the following figures: wages of $14,648, tips of $943, and $83 in interest income. You are not a dependent on your parents' return. Federal income tax in the amount of $1,248 was withheld. Use the table below to find the tax that is due (line 11). Sign your return.

6,000

6,000	6,050	603	603
6,050	6,100	608	608
6,100	6,150	613	613
6,150	6,200	618	618
6,200	6,250	623	623
6,250	6,300	628	628
6,300	6,350	633	633
6,350	6,400	638	638
6,400	6,450	643	643
6,450	6,500	648	648
6,500	6,550	653	653
6,550	6,600	658	658
6,600	6,650	663	663
6,650	6,700	668	668
6,700	6,750	673	673
6,750	6,800	678	678
6,800	6,850	683	683
6,850	6,900	688	688
6,900	6,950	693	693
6,950	7,000	698	698

(Continued on next page)

   Chapter 19 Taxes, Taxation, and Retirement Planning

Activity 19-4   Filing a Tax Return

<table>
<tr><td colspan="2">Form
1040EZ</td><td>Department of the Treasury—Internal Revenue Service
**Income Tax Return for Single and
Joint Filers With No Dependents** (99)</td><td>**2011**</td><td>OMB No. 1545-0074</td></tr>
</table>

Your first name and initial	Last name		Your social security number
If a joint return, spouse's first name and initial	Last name		Spouse's social security number
Home address (number and street). If you have a P.O. box, see instructions.		Apt. no.	▲ Make sure the SSN(s) above are correct.
City, town or post office, state, and ZIP code. If you have a foreign address, also complete spaces below (see instructions).			**Presidential Election Campaign** Check here if you, or your spouse if filing jointly, want $3 to go to this fund. Checking a box below will not change your tax or refund. ☐ You ☐ Spouse
Foreign country name	Foreign province/county	Foreign postal code	

Income

Attach Form(s) W-2 here.

Enclose, but do not attach, any payment.

1	Wages, salaries, and tips. This should be shown in box 1 of your Form(s) W-2. Attach your Form(s) W-2.	**1**
2	Taxable interest. If the total is over $1,500, you cannot use Form 1040EZ.	**2**
3	Unemployment compensation and Alaska Permanent Fund dividends (see instructions).	**3**
4	Add lines 1, 2, and 3. This is your **adjusted gross income.**	**4**
5	If someone can claim you (or your spouse if a joint return) as a dependent, check the applicable box(es) below and enter the amount from the worksheet on back. ☐ You ☐ Spouse If no one can claim you (or your spouse if a joint return), enter $9,500 if **single;** $19,000 if **married filing jointly.** See back for explanation.	**5**
6	Subtract line 5 from line 4. If line 5 is larger than line 4, enter -0-. This is your **taxable income.** ▶	**6**

Payments, Credits, and Tax

7	Federal income tax withheld from Form(s) W-2 and 1099.	**7**
8a	**Earned income credit (EIC)** (see instructions).	**8a**
b	Nontaxable combat pay election. 8b	
9	Add lines 7 and 8a. These are your **total payments and credits.** ▶	**9**
10	**Tax.** Use the amount on **line 6 above** to find your tax in the tax table in the instructions. Then, enter the tax from the table on this line.	**10**

Refund

Have it directly deposited! See instructions and fill in 11b, 11c, and 11d or Form 8888.

11a	If line 9 is larger than line 10, subtract line 10 from line 9. This is your **refund.** If Form 8888 is attached, check here ▶ ☐	**11a**
▶ **b**	Routing number	▶ **c** Type: ☐ Checking ☐ Savings
▶ **d**	Account number	

Amount You Owe

12	If line 10 is larger than line 9, subtract line 9 from line 10. This is the **amount you owe.** For details on how to pay, see instructions. ▶	**12**

Third Party Designee

Do you want to allow another person to discuss this return with the IRS (see instructions)? ☐ **Yes.** Complete below. ☐ **No**

Designee's name ▶	Phone no. ▶	Personal identification number (PIN) ▶

Sign Here

Joint return? See instructions.

Keep a copy for your records.

Under penalties of perjury, I declare that I have examined this return and, to the best of my knowledge and belief, it is true, correct, and accurately lists all amounts and sources of income I received during the tax year. Declaration of preparer (other than the taxpayer) is based on all information of which the preparer has any knowledge.

Your signature	Date	Your occupation	Daytime phone number
Spouse's signature. If a joint return, **both** must sign.	Date	Spouse's occupation	If the IRS sent you an Identity Protection PIN, enter it here (see inst.)

Paid Preparer Use Only

Print/Type preparer's name	Preparer's signature	Date	Check ☐ if self-employed	PTIN
Firm's name ▶			Firm's EIN ▶	
Firm's address ▶			Phone no.	

For Disclosure, Privacy Act, and Paperwork Reduction Act Notice, see instructions.   Cat. No. 11329W   Form **1040EZ** (2011)

Chapter 19 Taxes, Taxation, and Retirement Planning

Activity 19-5   Social Security Coverage

Circle the letter T for each true statement and the letter F for each false statement.

T   F   1. An insured worker can retire at age 62 with full benefits.

T   F   2. The spouse of a retired worker can receive retirement benefits.

T   F   3. The age at which you can retire with full benefits is scheduled to be reduced from 65 to 62.

T   F   4. Retirement payments are the best-known program in the federal Social Security system.

T   F   5. Payments received by a dependent upon the death of an insured worker are called survivors benefits.

T   F   6. Survivors benefits may include both a lump-sum payment and a monthly benefit.

T   F   7. Only the spouse of a deceased worker can receive survivors' benefits.

T   F   8. Payments made to an insured worker who is unable to work because of illness are called disability payments.

T   F   9. Disability payments are made only for physical disability.

T   F   10. Disability payments can begin one month after an individual becomes unable to work.

T   F   11. A spouse and other dependents are eligible for disability payments.

T   F   12. Hospital and medical insurance (Medicare) coverage begins at age 55.

T   F   13. Medicare pays 100 percent of all hospital expenses.

T   F   14. The medical coverage part of Medicare is an optional health insurance plan.

T   F   15. Unemployment insurance provides cash payments to workers who have lost their job.

T   F   16. Unemployment insurance benefits vary from state to state.

T   F   17. While receiving unemployment benefits, a worker can choose not to accept a suitable job offered by the state employment service.

T   F   18. Workers' compensation is to help individuals who become ill or injured as a result of their job.

T   F   19. Workers' compensation typically covers farm and household workers.

T   F   20. Workers' compensation laws are the same in all 50 states.

                    Chapter 19 Taxes, Taxation, and Retirement Planning

Activity 19-6 Administration and Financing of Social Security

1. What is the difference between public assistance and social insurance programs regarding how they are financed? ____

   ____

   ____

2. Who administers the six types of social insurance programs? _____________________________

   ____

   ____

3. The term *employment security* is sometimes used to describe unemployment benefits and

   workers' compensation programs. Explain why this is an appropriate label. ________________

   ____

   ____

4. Answer the following questions in relation to the current calendar year. (Visit the Social
   Security website at **http://www.ssa.gov** or contact a Social Security office to get up-to-date
   information.)

   a. How many work credits are required to be a *currently insured* worker? ________________

   b. How many work credits are required to be a *fully insured* worker? __________________

   c. How much do you have to earn a year to receive four work credits? __________________

   d. How much is the current wage base? ____

   e. What is the current FICA tax rate for employed workers? ___________________________

5. Compute the amount of FICA tax you would have to pay on the following annual earnings:

   $15,000 _______________ $20,000 ____________ $25,000 ____________

   $35,000 _______________ $50,000 ____________ $75,000 ____________

Activity 19-7   Individual Retirement Accounts

If you are qualified, you can set up an individual retirement account (IRA), contribute up to $5,000 a year, and deduct the amount you contributed from your gross income when figuring your income taxes. Complete the following exercise to see how much you could save in taxes. Use a federal income tax table for the current year to find "Tax."

	$15,000	$20,000	$25,000	$35,000	$50,000
Taxable income:					
Tax:	_______	_______	_______	_______	_______
Taxable income with IRA Contribution (Taxable income − $5,000):	_______	_______	_______	_______	_______
Revised tax:	_______	_______	_______	_______	_______
Tax savings (tax − revised tax):	_______	_______	_______	_______	_______
Actual cost of IRA contribution ($5,000 − tax savings):	_______	_______	_______	_______	_______

1. What does this exercise show regarding the tax-saving benefits of an IRA? ___________

   ____

   ____

   ____

2. How do our economy and our society benefit from the accumulation of IRA deposits?

   ____

   ____

   ____

3. For young adults with most of their work life ahead of them, which type(s) of investment(s) (stocks, bonds, mutual funds, certificates of deposit) would be most appropriate? Explain why.

   ____

   ____

   ____

Chapter 20   The Legal System

20-1   The Nature of Law

Activity 20-1   **Civil and Public Law**
Objective: To identify examples of civil and public law and explain the basic nature of each type

20-2   The Court System

Activity 20-2   **The Nature of Law**
Objective: To identify terms and concepts associated with law and law enforcement

Activity 20-3   **Types of Courts**
Objective: To identify and explain the types and roles of courts located in your region

20-3   Legal Services

Activity 20-4   **Small Claims Court**
Objective: describe the nature and role of small claims court

Activity 20-1   Civil and Public Law

Match the type of civil or public law with specific cases.

a. Civil law

b. Public law

______ 1. A person intentionally underpays federal income taxes.

______ 2. A retail clerk steals credit card numbers and sells them.

______ 3. A merchant sells a faulty product and refuses to exchange it.

______ 4. Congress passes legislation that may be unconstitutional.

______ 5. A roofing contractor fails to use the agreed upon materials.

______ 6. A married couple is in the process of adopting a baby.

______ 7. A stock fund manager cheats investors out of millions of dollars.

______ 8. Parties in a divorce disagree over custody arrangements for their children.

______ 9. A person is arrested for driving under the influence of alcohol.

______ 10. Two family members are in a dispute over who owns a piece of inherited property.

______ 11. A state is challenging the legality of a federal environmental law.

______ 12. Someone copies a song that you originally wrote.

Answer the following questions regarding the nature of civil and public law.

13. Explain the basic difference between civil and public law. _________________________

____

____

____

14. Case study #1: For the county in which you live, go online and identify a recent civil law

case. Summarize the case including the final judgment. _________________________

____

____

15. Case study #2: For the county in which you live, go online and identify a recent public law

case. Summarize the case including the final verdict. _________________________

____

____

____

    Chapter 20 The Legal System

Activity 20-2   The Nature of Law

Complete the following crossword puzzle by identifying the correct terms having to do with law and law enforcement.

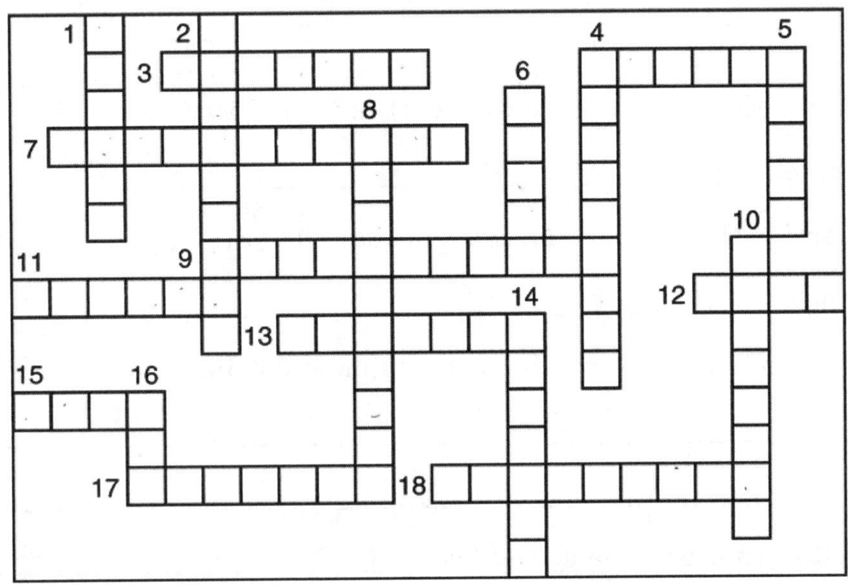

ACROSS

1. _______ attorney (lawyer who defends an accused person)

2. _______ law (defines rights and responsibilities under local, state, federal, and international law)

7. _______ attorney (lawyer who brings legal action against an accused person)

9. A hearing before a judge in which an arrested person is formally charged

11. _______ law (judge-made law)

12. Citizens who listen to the trial evidence and report their decision to a judge

13. A person who testifies at a trial

15. Money deposited with the court to guarantee a person will show up for trial

17. A court order authorizing a police officer to conduct a search, seizure, or arrest

18. Release of a convicted person under supervision and upon specified conditions

DOWN

1. A court order

2. The person against whom a court complaint or action is filed

4. The complaining party in a court case

5. _______ law (private law)

6. The person who presides over a court of law

8. A formal statement charging a person with an offense

10. A judge's decision

14. An order to appear in court

16. The body of enforced rules by which people live together

Chapter 20 The Legal System

Activity 20-3   Types of Courts

Answer these questions about types of courts found in your geographic area. You may need to do research at a library or online for the third question.

1. What is the name of the local court/lower court in your city or county? _________________

   Where is it located? ____

2. What is the name of the general trial court in your city or county? _________________

   Where is it located? ____

3. What is the difference between receiving a citation and being arrested? _______________

   ____

   ____

4. In which U.S. district court area do you live? ___________________________________

   Where is the court located? ____

5. For each of the following situations, identify the type of court in your geographic area in which the case would be resolved.

   a. A person is arrested for speeding: ____

   b. A person is arrested for burglary: ____

   c. A person is charged with destroying a mailbox: ____________________________

   d. A 14-year-old is charged with breaking a store window: ____________________

   e. A couple is adopting a baby: ____

   f. A person is cited for violating the city or county ordinance against burning leaves:

   ____

Chapter 20 The Legal System

Activity 20-4   Small Claims Court

Obtain a copy of written guidelines regarding small claims court in your area. Answer these questions.

1. Why is small claims court sometimes referred to as the people's court?

   ____

   ____

   ____

2. Where is the small claims court located in your geographic area? _______________________

   ____

3. Provide three examples of complaints for which a suit might be filed in a small claims court.

   a. ____

   ____

   ____

   b. ____

   ____

   ____

   c. ____

   ____

   ____

4. What is the maximum amount of money that can be recovered from small claims court in

   your state? ____

5. Briefly outline the steps to follow in filing a suit in small claims court. ________________

   ____

   ____

   ____

   ____

Chapter 20 The Legal System   **175**

Chapter 21 Where to Live

21-1 A Housing Plan

Activity 21-1   **Housing Needs and Wants**
Objective: To consider your housing needs and wants

21-2 Apartment Life

Activity 21-2   **Rental Agreement**
Objective: To explain the meaning of various statements often found
in apartment leases

Activity 21-3   **Tenant Relationships**
Objective: To explain how to deal with various tenant relationship
problems and situations

Activity 21-1 Housing Needs and Wants

1. How important to your overall lifestyle is a place to live? Explain. _______________________

____

____

____

2. Assume that you and a friend are going to share an apartment. List below those things that

   you need and want in housing. ____

____

____

____

3. Look through newspaper classified ads or on the Web for apartment rentals. How much
   does it appear that you might have to pay for an apartment that meets your needs and
   wants? What types of extras are often emphasized in apartment rental ads to attract young
   tenants?

____

____

____

____

4. Let us say that the type of apartment you need and want is not available or affordable.

   What things would you be most willing to give up? _____________________________________

____

____

____

Activity 21-2 Rental Agreement

The following statements were found in a rental agreement. Explain the meaning of each statement.

1. The Tenant accepts the premises in working order and agrees to clean and maintain the premises and to yield the premises at the end of the said lease period in the same condition, ordinary wear and tear excepted. ____

   ____

   ____

   ____

   ____

2. The Tenant agrees not to make any structural changes or cosmetic alterations on or about the said property without the previous written consent of the Lessor. _______________

   ____

   ____

   ____

   ____

3. Upon execution of this agreement, the Tenant shall pay the Lessor a security deposit equal to the amount shown. ____

   ____

   ____

   ____

   ____

4. The Lessor and/or the Lessor's agent shall have the right to enter the premises at reasonable hours to make inspections or repairs. _______________________________

   ____

   ____

   ____

   ____

(Continued on next page)

Chapter 21 Where to Live

Activity 21-2 Rental Agreement

5. The Tenant agrees not to assign this lease without the written consent of the Lessor.

____

____

____

6. The Lessor is not liable for any damages to the personal belongings of the Tenant. _______

____

____

____

7. If the Tenant shall be in default of any of the covenants on his or her part, the Lessor

   shall have the right to terminate the tenancy. _________________________________

____

____

____

____

8. The Lessor shall have the right to terminate the tenancy where neither party is in default
   upon delivering a notice specifying the Lessor's election to terminate. (month-to-month
   rental)

____

____

____

____

Chapter 21 Where to Live

Activity 21-3 Tenant Relationships

Living in an apartment complex with dozens or hundreds of other tenants often presents difficult problems in tenant relationships. Explain how you would handle each of these situations.

1. When you come home from work, other tenants or guests are often parked in your reserved space. ____

   ____

   ____

   ____

2. Whenever you go to the pool to sunbathe, someone always seems to come over to chat. Most tenants are very nice, but you would really like to be left alone. ___________________

   ____

   ____

   ____

3. The couple down the hall cooks foods that are unfamiliar to you. Sometimes when you step out into the hallway, the smell almost makes you sick. _________________________________

   ____

   ____

   ____

4. One of your neighbors is always borrowing an egg, a stick of margarine, a cup of milk, or the like. Very seldom does he pay you back. _______________________________________

   ____

   ____

   ____

5. Tenants are not allowed to have pets. However, you frequently hear a puppy barking in the apartment across the hall. ____

   ____

   ____

   ____

(Continued on next page)

    Chapter 21 Where to Live

Activity 21-3 Tenant Relationships

6. You have lived in the apartment for several months but have not made any new friends. Everyone seems to be so busy. ____

____

____

____

7. You often notice a person who seems to be watching your apartment. It makes you feel very uncomfortable. ____

____

____

____

8. One of your neighbors has an infant. She often asks you if you would mind keeping your door open to listen for the baby while she runs an errand. ____

____

____

9. Since your neighbors are not home, a delivery person asks if you will accept and sign for delivery of a small package. ____

____

____

10. A new couple is moving into the corner apartment. They have been hauling their belongings all day and look absolutely beat. ____

____

____

____

Chapter 21 Where to Live

Chapter 22   The Rest of Your Life

22-1   Be a Citizen

Activity 22-1   **The Nature of Citizenship**
Objective: To name terms or concepts associated with citizenship

Activity 22-2   **Elections and Voting**
Objective: To answer questions regarding eclection and voting procedures and requirements in your city and state

22-2   Think Clearly

Activity 22-3   **Evaluating Propaganda**
Objective: To critique a piece of propaganda

22-3   Education and Training Options

Activity 22-4   **Evaluating Educational Alternatives**
Objective: To obtain descriptive information regarding an education or training alternative of interest

22-4   Educational and Financial Aid Information

Activity 22-5   **Seeking Educational Information**
Objective: To practice writing a letter requesting information about education or training requirements and opportunities

Activity 22-1 The Nature of Citizenship

Complete the following word puzzle by filling in the correct terms.

							C				
1							I				
2							T				
3							I				
4							Z				
5							E				
6							N				
7							S				
8							H				
9							I				
10							P				

1. Good citizenship helps preserve this form of government.

2. Citizenship is acquired primarily by this process.

3. The legal basis for citizenship is contained in this document.

4. The special legal process of becoming a citizen

5. A person who holds the legal position of citizenship

6. People can serve the government by contributing to the national _____________________.

7. This type of citizenship activity involves producing efficiently and consuming wisely.

8. This type of citizenship activity involves preserving basic social institutions and adhering to the customs and laws of society.

9. A pledge of loyalty to the United States taken at a naturalization ceremony

10. This type of citizenship activity involves being informed on issues and voting during elections.

11. To share in the duties and responsibilities of citizenship

Chapter 22 The Rest of Your Life   183

Activity 22-2 Elections and Voting

Answer the questions regarding types of elections and voting procedures and requirements.

1. Does your state have a **closed** or **open** primary election? _______________________________

2. Does your state have a Presidential primary or caucus? _________________________________

   If so, explain how and when it is conducted. ____

   ____

   ____

   ____

3. What are the residency requirements regarding the following types of elections?

   a. National: ____

   b. State: ____

   c. Local: ____

   ____

4. Provide an example of a special election that has been held in your state or community.

   ____

   ____

   ____

5. Where do you go to obtain an absentee ballot in your city or county? ________________________

   Describe the procedure for casting an absentee ballot. ____________________________________

   ____

   ____

6. Why do you think that fewer than 40 percent of 18- to 20-year-olds vote in a general

   election?____

   ____

7. Have you registered to vote, or do you plan to register? _______________ Why or why not?

   ____

   ____

   ____

　　　　　　　　　　　　　　　　　Chapter 22 The Rest of Your Life

Activity 22-3 Evaluating Propaganda

Propaganda appears in magazines, in newspapers, on TV, on the radio, and on the Web. You see it on billboards and bulletin boards. It arrives by mail and is passed out by people in the street. Obtain a statement of propaganda, or record notes about something you saw or heard. Identify the type of propaganda (pamphlet, magazine ad, television commercial, or other type) and explain how you became aware of it (arrived in the mail, picked up at the mall, etc.):

____

Now, answer the following questions about the propaganda.

1. What is the primary message contained in the propaganda? ______________________________

____

____

____

2 Are you being urged to take some kind of action? ______________ If so, what? ________

____

____

3. What person or group is putting out the propaganda? ___________________________________

____

4. Why do you think the person or group wants you to believe the propaganda? ____________

____

____

5. What is the opposing argument or point of view? ______________________________________

____

____

6. In your opinion, is the propaganda good or bad? ______________ Explain your opinion:

____

____

____

____

Chapter 22 The Rest of Your Life   **185**

Activity 22-4 Evaluating Educational Alternatives

Identify a technical school, community college, college, or other education or training alternative in which you are interested. Contact the institution or use one of the sources of education and training information listed in Chapter 22 to obtain the information requested below.

1. Name of occupation for which training is desired ____

2. Name of program, major, or specialization ____

3. What type of degree, certificate, or other credentials will be received after completion of

   the program? ____

4. What are the entrance requirements? ____

5. How long does it take to complete the program? ____

   ____

6. How much does the program cost per year or total (specify)?

   ■ Tuition _______________

   ■ Fees _______________

   ■ Books and supplies _______________

   ■ Room and board _______________

7. Is any financial aid available? _______________ If so, explain: _______________

   ____

   ____

   ____

8. Does the institution provide job placement services? _______________ If so, explain:

   ____

   ____

   ____

   ____

     Chapter 22 The Rest of Your Life

Activity 22-5 Seeking Educational Information

As part of Activity 1-7, you identified "Sources of Additional Information" for an occupation of interest. Select one of the sources and write an appropriate letter requesting information about education and training requirements and opportunities.

____

____

____

____

____

____

Dear_____________________________________

____

____

____

____

____

____

____

____

____

____

Sincerely

____

Part 2
EXPLORING CAREER CLUSTERS

This part contains 16 Career Clusters ™ based on the Standard Occupational Classification (SOC) and the North American Industry Classification System (NAICS). The framework for the clusters was first proposed by the U.S. Department of Education's Office of Vocational and Adult Education in November 1999. The National Career Clusters™ Framework is currently supported by the National Association of State Directors of Career Technical Education Consortium (*www.careertech.org/ career-clusters*).

Within each cluster, related occupations contained in the 2012–13 Edition of the *Occupational Outlook Handbook (OOH)* are listed. The SOC number accompanies each specific occupational title followed by a short description condensed from the *OOH*. A total of 341 occupational titles and descriptions are provided in Part 2, which comprise about 85 percent of total U.S. employment. The *OOH* does not contain descriptions of hundreds of other important, but minor, occupations. However, a comprehensive listing of occupations classified according to the 16 Career Clusters™ may be found at O*NET (*www.onetonline.org/find/career*).

Part 2 begins with a brief explanation on pages 190–193 of how to interpret occupational information in the *OOH* and a sample occupational description on page 194. This information is reproduced verbatim from the *OOH*. This section concludes on pages 246–247 with a copy of the form contained in Activity 1-11, which is suitable for reproduction.

1. Agriculture, Food & Natural Resources
2. Architecture & Construction
3. Arts, Audio/Video Technology & Communications
4. Business Management & Administration
5. Education & Training
6. Finance
7. Government & Public Administration
8. Health Science
9. Hospitality & Tourism
10. Human Services
11. Information Technology
12. Law, Public Safety, Corrections & Security
13. Manufacturing
14. Marketing
15. Science, Technology, Engineering & Mathematics
16. Transportation, Distribution & Logistics

Occupational Information Included in the *OOH*

The *Occupational Outlook Handbook (OOH)* is a career guidance resource offering information on the hundreds of occupations that provide the overwhelming majority of jobs in the United States. Each occupational profile discusses what workers in that occupation do, their work environment, the typical education and training needed to enter the occupation, pay, and the job outlook for the occupation. Each profile is in a standard format that makes it easy to compare occupations.

This page describes the content found in each occupational profile.

Sections of Occupational Profiles

- Summary
- What They Do
- Work Environment
- How to Become One
- Pay
- Job Outlook
- Similar Occupations
- Contacts for More Information

Summary

All profiles have a "Quick Facts" table that gives information on the following topics:

2010 Median Pay: The wage at which half of the workers in the occupation earned more than that amount and half earned less. Median wage data are from the BLS Occupational Employment Statistics survey.

Entry-Level Education: Typical level of education that most workers need to enter the occupation.

Work Experience in a Related Occupation: Work experience that is commonly considered necessary by employers or is a commonly accepted substitute for more formal types of training or education.

On-the-job Training: Postemployment training necessary to attain competency in the skills needed in the occupation.

Number of Jobs, 2010: The employment, or size, of this occupation in 2010, the base year of the 2010–20 employment projections.

Job Outlook, 2010–20: The projected rate of change in employment for the 10-year timeframe between 2010 and 2020. The average growth rate for all occupations is 14.3 percent.

Employment Change, 2010–20: The projected numeric change in employment for this occupation between 2010 and 2020.

The summary section briefly describes all of the sections included in each occupational profile. In addition, a link is given to the Occupational Information Network (O*NET) system. State employment service offices use O*NET to classify applicants and job openings. For each occupation, O*NET lists descriptors, including common tasks, necessary knowledge and skills, and frequently used technology.

What They Do

This section describes the main work of people in the occupation.

All occupations have a list of duties or typical tasks performed by these workers. The list includes daily responsibilities, such as answering phone calls and taking a patient's medical history.

This section also may describe the equipment, tools, software, or other items that are typically used by people in the occupation. For example, medical records and health information technicians frequently use electronic health records to document a patient's medical information. This section also may describe those with whom workers in the occupation interact, such as clients, patients, and coworkers.

Some profiles discuss specific specialties, job titles, or types of occupations within a given occupation. This subsection includes a brief explanation of each specialty's job duties and how specialties differ from one another. For example, the profile on dentists lists several specialties, including orthodontists, oral and maxillofacial surgeons, and pediatric dentists.

Work Environment

This section describes an occupation's working conditions, including the workplace, expected level of physical activity, and typical hours.

The section typically begins by noting the employment size of the occupation in 2010 and often includes a table of the industries or settings that employed the most workers in an occupation that year. The workplace is described, and whether employees work in a safe work environment (such as an office) or a hazardous one (such as a commercial fishing boat) is discussed. If the workplace is hazardous, the section lists the type of equipment an employee must wear, such as a lab coat or protective goggles. In addition to information on the general work environment, the section also notes whether employees are expected to travel, and, if so, for how long.

The section includes information on the typical schedule for workers in an occupation, noting whether the majority of workers are employed full time or part time. Full-time workers typically work 35 or more hours in a week, whereas part-time employees work less than 35 hours. For some occupations, the profile might also include the time of a day an employee is expected to work and for how long. Nurses, for example, may work all hours of the day and on weekends, because medical facilities are open around the clock. Information on occupations, such as farmers, that have seasonal employment also can be found in this section.

How to Become One

This section describes the typical paths to entry into, and advancement in, an occupation. All profiles have subsections on education and on important qualities of workers in the occupation. Optional subsections include information on training, work experience, licenses, certification, and advancement.

Education

This subsection describes the education that most workers typically need to enter an occupation. Some occupations require no formal education, whereas others may require, for example, a doctoral degree or Ph.D. In some occupations, such as computer support specialist, workers have varying educational backgrounds. In these cases, the profile will discuss all of the typical paths of entry into the occupation.

This subsection also may include information on what subjects, majors, or minors people study in preparation for the occupation. Typical courses that may aid a student in preparing for an occupation may be listed. For example, high school students interested in applying to respiratory therapy programs should take courses in health, biology, mathematics, chemistry, and physics.

Work experience

This subsection describes whether employers require work experience in a related occupation. For example, some managers, such as architectural and engineering managers, typically have previous work experience as an architect or engineer.

Training

This subsection describes the typical on-the-job training necessary to attain competency in an occupation. Information is included on any practical or classroom training that workers receive after being hired. For example, firefighters must complete training at a fire academy or a similar program before they are considered prepared to combat fires.

In these profiles, apprenticeships and internship or residency programs are considered on-the-job training. For example, the profile on physicians and surgeons includes information on residency programs.

Licenses

This subsection describes whether licensing is typically needed for an occupation and, if so, how workers can become licensed.

Licenses are issued by states to signify that the person has met specific legal requirements to practice that occupation. To become licensed, workers usually need to pass an examination and comply with eligibility requirements, such as possessing a minimum level of education, work experience, or training, or completing an internship, a residency, or a formal apprenticeship. States have their own regulatory boards that set standards for practicing a licensed occupation, so rules and eligibility may vary from state to state, even for the same occupation.

Certification

This subsection describes whether workers in an occupation are typically certified and, if so, how they can become certified.

Some occupations have certification either as a requirement or as a nonrequired opportunity. As an example of the latter, fitness trainers and instructors are encouraged, not required, to become certified before entering the occupation, and employers will often allow a trainer or instructor to become certified after being hired.

Certification requires demonstrated competency in a skill or a set of skills and is commonly earned by passing an examination or having a certain amount and type of work experience or training. For some certification programs, the candidate must have a certain level of education before becoming eligible for certification. This subsection explains any prerequisites to certification and how a person would complete certification (by passing an exam, performing a certain type of work, receiving certain training or education, etc.). If states require workers to be certified before they can be licensed, that information also is noted here.

Certification should not be confused with certificates from an educational institution. A certificate awarded by a postsecondary educational institution is considered to be a postsecondary nondegree award and would be discussed in the subsection on education.

Important qualities

This subsection describes important characteristics of workers in the occupation and includes an explanation of why those characteristics are useful.

The qualities include areas of skills, aptitudes, and personal characteristics. For example, an emergency medical technician or paramedic must be physically strong, and a medical laboratory technologist or technician relies on technical skills to complete laboratory work.

Advancement

This subsection describes the possible advancement opportunities for workers in the occupation.

Opportunities for advancement can come from within the occupation, such as a promotion to a supervisory or managerial level; advancement into another occupation, such as moving from a computer support specialist to a network and computer systems administrator; or becoming self-employed, such as a dentist opening up his or her own practice.

The section often explains the requirements for advancement, such as certification or additional formal education.

Pay

This section discusses the wages of workers in the occupation.

For each occupation, pay varies by experience, responsibility, performance, tenure, and geographic area. Almost all occupations discussed in the OOH use median wage data from the Occupational Employment Statistics (OES) survey, which provides data on wage and salary workers.

The median wage is the wage at which half of the workers in an occupation earned more and half earned less. This section might also include wages earned by workers in selected industries—those in which most of an occupation's workers are employed. The wage data by industry are also from the OES survey.

For all occupations for which OES survey data are used, the profile includes median wages and the wages earned by the top 10 percent and bottom 10 percent of workers in the occupation. The wage data are accompanied by a chart comparing the median wage of workers in the occupation to the median wage of workers across all occupations.

Unless otherwise noted, the source of pay data for occupations in the *OOH* is the Bureau of Labor Statistics. Some occupational profiles may cite wage data from sources other than the BLS. For example, wage data on physicians and surgeons is provided by the Medical Group Management Association.

Work schedule information, also found in the "Work Environment" section, is provided again here, and, if notable, this section might include the percentage of an occupation's workers who are members of a union.

Job Outlook

This section describes how employment will grow or decline between 2010 and 2020. Growth rates are from the 2010–20 occupational projections from the National Employment Matrix. In addition to presenting projections data, the outlook section cites major factors affecting the growth or decline of employment. Some common factors in employment growth or decline are industry growth or decline, technological change, fluctuating demand for a product or service, demographic change, or changes in business practices.

The outlook section sometimes also includes a "job prospects" subsection, which provides a qualitative measure of job competition.

Similar Occupations

This section links to other occupational profiles with similar job duties or required skills.

Contacts for More Information

This section includes external links to associations, organizations, and other institutions that may provide readers with additional information.

Key Phrases in the OOH

The following table explains how to interpret the key phrases used to describe projected changes in employment:

Changing employment between 2010 and 2020

If the statement reads:	Employment is projected to:
Grow much faster than average	increase 29 percent or more
Grow faster than average	increase 20 to 28 percent
Grow about as fast as average	increase 10 to 19 percent
Grow more slowly than average	increase 3 to 9 percent
Little or no change	decrease 2 percent to increase 2 percent
Decline slowly or moderately	decrease 3 to 9 percent
Decline rapidly	decrease 10 percent or more

Retail Sales Workers

Summary

Quick Facts: Retail Sales Workers	
2010 Median Pay	$20,990 per year $10.09 per hour
Entry-Level Education	Less than high school
Work Experience in a Related Occupation	None
On-the-job Training	*See* How to Become One
Number of Jobs, 2010	4,465,500
Job Outlook, 2010–20	17% (About as fast as average)
Employment Change, 2010–20	739,400

What Retail Sales Workers Do

Retail sales workers include both those who sell retail merchandise, such as clothing, furniture, and automobiles, (called retail salespersons) and those who sell spare and replacement parts and equipment, especially car parts, (called parts salespersons). Both groups help customers find the products they want and process customers' payments.

Work Environment

Most retail sales workers work in clean, comfortable, well-lit stores. Many sales workers work evenings and weekends. More than one-third of retail salespersons work part time.

How to Become a Retail Sales Worker

Typically, retail sales workers do not need a formal education. However, some employers prefer applicants who have a high school diploma or equivalent.

Pay

The median hourly wage of retail salespersons was $9.94 in May 2010. The median hourly wage of parts salespersons was $13.88 in May 2010.

Job Outlook

Employment of retail salespersons is expected to grow 17 percent from 2010 to 2020, about as fast as the average for all occupations. Employment of parts salespersons is expected to grow 16 percent from 2010 to 2020, about as fast as the average for all occupations. Many workers leave this occupation, which means there will be a large number of job openings. This large number of job openings combined with the large size of the occupation should result in many employment opportunities.

Similar Occupations

Compare the job duties, education, job growth, and pay of retail sales workers with similar occupations.

O*NET

O*NET provides comprehensive information on key characteristics of workers and occupations.

Contacts for More Information

Learn more about retail sales workers by contacting these additional resources.

1. AGRICULTURE, FOOD, AND NATURAL RESOURCES

Workers in agriculture, food and natural resources occupations provide many of the raw materials used to satisfy our basic needs for food, shelter, and clothing. These are the growers and gatherers that depend largely on the resources of nature for their livelihood. Agriculture workers raise plants and animals that provide us with food and fiber (such as wool and cotton). Forestry workers harvest trees that provide lumber for buildings and furniture construction as well as pulp for a variety of paper products. Fishers gather marine and animal life that is eaten and used in fertilizer and other products. Extractive workers mine the fuels and other raw materials needed for heat and power and used in manufacturing, construction, and agriculture. The work of these growers and gatherers are aided and supervised by a number of agricultural managers, conservation scientists and foresters, and mining and petroleum engineers. Another group of highly trained scientists and technicians work on solutions to producing and processing food; extracting oil, gas, and minerals; and protecting and preserving the environment.

The following occupations are included in the Agriculture, Food and Natural Resources Career Cluster. For further information about a specific occupation go to *www.bls.gov/ooh/* and key the name of the occupation in the search window.

Agricultural and Food Scientists (19-1010)

Agricultural and food scientists play an important role in maintaining the nation's food supply. Many work in basic or applied research and development. Basic research seeks to understand the biological and chemical processes by which crops and livestock grow. Applied research uses this knowledge to discover ways to improve the quality, quantity, and safety of agricultural products.

Agricultural and Food Science Technicians (19-4011)

Under the supervision of scientists, agricultural and food science technicians measure and analyze the quality of food and agricultural products. Agricultural technicians who work in private industry focus on the condition of crops and animals, not on processed foods. Food science technicians who work in private industry inspect food and crops, including processed food, to ensure the product is fit for distribution.

Agricultural Engineers (17-2021)

Agricultural engineers—also known as biological and agricultural engineers—work on a variety of activities. These activities range from aquaculture (raising food, such as fish, that thrive in water) to land farming to forestry; from developing biofuels to improving conservation; from planning animal environments to finding better ways to process food.

Agricultural Workers (45-2021, 2090)

Agricultural workers maintain the quality of farms, crops, and livestock by operating machinery and doing physical labor under the supervision of agricultural managers. Some agricultural workers, also called migrant farm workers, move from location to location as crops ripen.

Conservation Scientists and Foresters (19-1030)

Conservation scientists and foresters manage overall land quality of forests, parks, rangelands, and other natural resources. Many conservation scientists and foresters supervise forest and conservation workers and technicians, directing their work and evaluating their progress.

Environmental Engineers
(17-2081)

Environmental engineers use the principles of engineering, soil science, biology, and chemistry to develop solutions to environmental problems. They are involved in efforts to improve recycling, waste disposal, public health, and control of water and air pollution. They also address global issues, such as safe drinking water, climate change, and sustainability.

Environmental Engineering Technicians
(17-3025)

Environmental engineering technicians carry out the plans that environmental engineers develop. They test, operate, and, if necessary, modify equipment for preventing or cleaning up environmental pollution. They may collect samples for testing, or they may work to mitigate sources of environmental pollution.

Environmental Science and Protection Technicians (19-4091)

Environmental science and protection technicians do laboratory and field tests to monitor the environment and investigate sources of pollution, including those affecting health. Many work under the supervision of environmental scientists and specialists, who direct their work and evaluate their results.

Environmental Scientists and Specialists
(19-2041)

Environmental scientists and specialists use their knowledge of the natural sciences to protect the environment. They identify problems and find solutions that minimize hazards to the health of the environment and the population.

Farmers, Ranchers, and Other Agricultural Managers (11-9013)

Farmers, ranchers, and other agricultural managers run establishments that produce crops, livestock, and dairy products. On very large farms, farmers, ranchers, and other agricultural mangers may spend a lot of time meeting with farm supervisors. Professional agricultural managers overseeing several farms may divide their time between traveling to meet farmers and planning operations in their offices.

Fishers and Related Fishing Workers
(45-3011)

Fishers and related fishing workers catch and trap various types of marine life. The fish they catch are for human food, animal feed, bait, and other uses. Some fishers work in deep water on large fishing boats that are equipped for long stays at sea. Some process the fish they catch on board and prepare them for sale. Other fishers work in shallow water on small boats that often have a crew of only one or two members.

Forest and Conservation Technicians
(19-4093)

Forest and conservation technicians measure and improve the quality of forests, rangeland, and other natural areas. Forest and conservation technicians generally work under the supervision of foresters or conservation scientists. Increasing numbers of forest and conservation technicians work in urban forestry and other nontraditional specialties, rather than in forests or rural areas.

Forest and Conservation Workers (45-4011)

Under the supervision of foresters and forest and conservation technicians, forest and conservation workers help to develop, maintain, and protect forests. They do basic tasks such as planting seedlings or removing diseased trees. Some forest workers work on tree farms, where they plant, cultivate, and harvest many different kinds of trees.

Geological and Petroleum Technicians
(19-4041)

Geological and petroleum technicians provide support to scientists and engineers in exploring and extracting natural resources, such as minerals, oil, and natural gas. In the field, they use sophisticated equipment such as seismic instruments and gravity-measuring devices to gather geological data. They also use hand tools to collect samples of rocks and other materials for scientific analysis.

Geoscientists (19-2042)

Geoscientists study the physical aspects of the Earth, such as its composition, structure, and processes, to learn about its past, present, and future. Many geoscientists are involved in the search for and development of natural resources and minerals such as petroleum. Others work in environmental protection and preservation and are involved in projects to clean up and reclaim land.

Hydrologists (19-2043)

Hydrologists study water and the water cycle. They study the movement, distribution, and other properties of water, and they analyze how these influence the surrounding environment. They use their expertise to solve problems concerning water quality and availability.

Logging Workers (45-4020)

Logging workers harvest thousands of acres of forests each year. The timber they harvest provides the raw material for countless consumer and industrial products. Timber-cutting and logging are done by a logging crew having many different titles such as fallers, buckers, chock setters, and logging equipment operators.

Mining and Geological Engineers (17-2151)

Mining and geological engineers design mines for the safe and efficient removal of minerals, such as coal and metals, for manufacturing and utilities. They often work at mining operations in remote locations. However, some work in sand-and-gravel operations that are located near larger cities.

Oil and Gas Workers (47-5010, 5071)

Oil and gas workers carry out the plans for drilling that petroleum engineers have designed. Drilling workers operate the equipment that drills the well through the soil and rock formation, and they prepare the well for use. Service workers then finish preparing the well and assemble the equipment that removes the oil or gas from the well.

Petroleum Engineers (17-2171)

Oil and gas deposits, or reservoirs, are located deep in rock formations underground. These reservoirs can only be accessed by drilling wells, either on land or at sea from off-shore oil rigs. Petroleum engineers design and develop methods for extracting oil and gas from deposits below the earth's surface. Petroleum engineers also find new ways to extract oil and gas from older wells.

Zoologists and Wildlife Biologists (19-1023)

Zoologists and wildlife biologists study the characteristics and habitats of animals and wildlife. They use geographic information systems, modeling software, and other computer programs to estimate populations and track the behavior patterns of animals. They also use these programs to forecast the spread of invasive species, diseases, and other potential threats to wildlife.

2. ARCHITECTURE AND CONSTRUCTION

Most construction projects require a team effort. This cluster includes occupations that plan, design, construct, remodel, and beautify houses, factories, offices, stores, schools, highways, and other structures and projects. Architects plan and design construction projects, while surveyors lay out the boundaries of the project and the land it occupies. Heavy equipment operators clear and prepare the site for construction. Dozens of different skilled workers including cement masons, carpenters, electricians, plumbers, and painters erect and finish the construction project. These types of occupations are often referred to as the building trades. Some occupations specialize in construction of commercial buildings and public works such as highways, bridges, and sewers.

The following occupations are included in the Architecture and Construction Career Cluster. For further information about a specific occupation go to *www.bls.gov /ooh/* and key the name of the occupation in the search window.

Architects (17-1011)

Architects plan and design buildings and other structures. People need places to live, work, play, learn, worship, meet, govern, shop, and eat. Architects are responsible for designing these places, whether they are private or public; indoors or outdoors; or rooms, buildings, or complexes.

Boilermakers (47-2011)

Boilers, tanks, and vats are used in many buildings, factories, and ships. Boilers heat water or other fluids under extreme pressure to generate electric power and to provide heat. Large tanks and vats are used to store and process chemicals, oil, beer, and hundreds of other products. Boilermakers assemble, install, and repair boilers, closed vats, and other large vessels or containers that hold liquids and gases.

Brickmasons, Blockmasons, and Stonemasons (47-2021, 2022)

Brickmasons, blockmasons, and stonemasons (or, simply, masons) use bricks, concrete blocks, and natural stones to build fences, walkways, walls, and other structures. Although most masons work in residential construction, nonresidential construction is growing in importance because most nonresidential buildings are now built with walls made of some combination of concrete block, brick veneer, stone, granite, marble, tile, and glass.

Carpenters (47-2031)

Carpenters are one of the most versatile construction occupations, with workers usually doing a variety of tasks. Carpenters construct and repair building frameworks and structures—such as stairways, doorframes, partitions, and rafters—made from wood and other materials. They also may install kitchen cabinets, siding, and drywall.

Carpet Installers (47-2041)

Carpet installers lay carpet in many types of new and old buildings, including homes, offices, restaurants, and museums. Although installing carpet in newly constructed buildings requires minimal preparation, those who replace existing carpet must first remove old flooring, including any padding, glue, tacks, or staples.

Cement Masons and Terrazzo Workers (47-2051, 2053)

Concrete is one of the most common and durable materials used in construction. Once set, concrete becomes the foundation for everything from decorative patios and floors to huge dams or miles of roadways. Cement masons pour, smooth, and finish concrete floors, sidewalks, roads, and curbs. Using a cement mixture, terrazzo workers create durable and decorative surfaces for floors and stairways.

Civil Engineering Technicians (17-3022)

Civil engineering technicians help civil engineers plan and design the construction of highways, bridges, utilities, and other major infrastructure projects. They also help with commercial, residential, and land development. Civil engineering technicians work under the direction of a licensed civil engineer.

Civil Engineers (17-2051)

Civil engineers design and supervise large construction projects, including roads, buildings, airports, tunnels, dams, bridges, and systems for water supply and sewage treatment. Many civil engineers hold supervisory or administrative positions ranging from supervisor of a construction site to city engineer. Others work in design, construction, research, and teaching.

Construction and Building Inspectors (47-4041)

Construction and building inspectors ensure that new construction, changes, or repairs comply with local and national building codes and ordinances, zoning regulations, and contract specifications. Although no two inspections are alike, inspectors do an initial check during the first phase of construction and follow-up inspections throughout the construction project. When the project is finished, they do a final, comprehensive inspection.

Construction Equipment Operators (47-2070)

Construction equipment operators use machinery to move construction materials, earth, and other heavy materials at construction sites and mines. They operate equipment that clears and grades land to prepare it for construction of roads, bridges, and buildings, as well as airport runways, power generation facilities, dams, levees, and other structures.

Construction Laborers and Helpers (47-2061)

Construction laborers and helpers do many basic tasks that require physical labor on construction sites. They perform a wide range of tasks from the very easy to the extremely difficult and hazardous. Although many of the tasks they do require some training and experience, most jobs usually require little skill and can be learned quickly.

Construction Managers (11-9021)

Construction managers, often called general contractors or project managers, coordinate and supervise a wide variety of projects, including the building of all types of residential, commercial, and industrial structures, roads, bridges, power plants, schools, and hospitals. Construction managers plan, coordinate, budget, and supervise construction projects from early development to completion.

Drafters (17-3010)

Drafters use software to convert the designs of engineers and architects into technical drawings and plans. Workers in production and construction use these plans to build everything from microchips to skyscrapers.

Drywall and Ceiling Tile Installers, and Tapers (47-2081, 2082)

Drywall and ceiling tile installers hang wallboards to walls and ceilings inside buildings. Tapers prepare the wallboards for painting, using tape and other materials. Many workers do both installing and taping.

Electricians (47-2111)

Almost every building has an electrical system that is installed during construction and maintained after that. Electricians do both the installing and maintaining of electrical systems. Many electricians work independently, but sometimes they collaborate with others. For example, experienced electricians may work with building engineers and architects to help design electrical systems in new construction.

Elevator Installers and Repairers (47-4021)

Elevator installers and repairers, also called elevator constructors or elevator mechanics, assemble, install, and replace elevators, escalators, chairlifts, moving walkways, and similar equipment in buildings. When the equipment is in service, they maintain and repair it. Elevator installers and repairers usually specialize in installation, maintenance, or repair work.

Glaziers (47-2121)

Glaziers install glass in windows, skylights, storefronts, and display cases to create distinctive designs or reduce the need for artificial lighting. In homes, glaziers install or replace windows, mirrors, shower doors, and bathtub enclosures. Glazing projects also may involve replacing storefront windows for supermarkets, auto dealerships, banks, and so on.

Hazardous Materials Removal Workers (47-4041)

Hazardous removal workers clean up materials (hazmat) that are harmful to people and the environment. Hazmat workers identify and dispose of asbestos, radioactive and nuclear waste, arsenic, lead, and other hazardous materials. They also clean up materials that are flammable, corrosive, reactive, or toxic.

Insulation Workers (47-2131, 2132)

Insulation workers install and replace the materials used to insulate buildings and their mechanical systems to help control and maintain temperature. Workers are often referred to as insulators. When renovating old buildings, insulators often must remove the old insulation.

Landscape Architects (17-2012)

Landscape architects plan and design land areas for parks, recreational facilities, highways, airports, and other properties. Projects include subdivisions and commercial, industrial, and residential sites. Many landscape architects specialize in a particular area, such as beautifying or otherwise improving streets and highways, waterfronts, parks and playgrounds, or shopping centers.

Painters, Construction and Maintenance (47-2141)

Painters apply paint, stain, and coatings to walls, buildings, bridges, and other structures. Because there are several ways to apply paint, workers must be able to choose the proper tool for each job, such as the correct roller, power sprayer, and the right size brush. Choosing the right tool typically depends on the surface to be covered and the characteristics of the finish.

Plasterers and Stucco Masons (47-2161)

Plasterers and stucco masons apply coats of plaster or stucco to walls, ceilings, or partitions for functional and decorative purposes. Using molds and a variety of troweling techniques, some plasterers make decorative and ornamental designs, which require special skills and creativity.

Plumbers, Pipefitters, and Steamfitters (47-2152)

Plumbers, pipefitters, and steamfitters install and repair pipes that carry water, steam, air, or other liquids or gases to and in businesses, homes, and factories. Although plumbers, pipefitters, and steamfitters are three distinct specialties, their duties are often similar.

Reinforcing Iron and Rebar Workers (47-2171)

Concrete is often used in construction. To reinforce the concrete, reinforcing iron and rebar workers install mesh, steel bars (rebar), or cables to reinforce concrete. Workers must be able to carry, bend, cut, and connect rebar at a rapid pace to keep projects on schedule.

Roofers (47-2181)

Roofers repair and install the roofs of buildings using a variety of materials, including shingles, asphalt, and metal. In northern states, roofing work is limited during the winter months. During the summer, roofers may work overtime to complete jobs quickly, especially before rainfall.

Sheet Metal Workers (47-2211)

Sheet metal workers make, install, and maintain thin sheet metal products. Although sheet metal is used to make many products, such as rain gutters, outdoor signs, and siding, it is most commonly used to make ducts for heating and air-conditioning.

Structural Iron and Steel Workers (47-2221)

Structural iron and steel workers install iron or steel beams, girders, and columns to form buildings, bridges, and other structures. They are often referred to as ironworkers. Some ironworkers make structural metal in fabricating shops, which are usually located away from the construction site.

Surveyors (17-1022)

Surveyors establish land, airspace, and water boundaries. They measure the Earth's surface to collect data that are used to draw maps, determine the shape and contour of parcels of land, and set property lines and boundaries. They also define airspace for airports and measure construction and mining sites. Surveyors work with civil engineers, landscape architects, and urban and regional planners to develop comprehensive design documents.

Surveying and Mapping Technicians (17-3031)

Surveying and mapping technicians assist surveyors and cartographers in collecting data and making maps of the earth's surface. Surveying technicians visit sites to take measurements of the land. Mapping technicians use geographic data to create maps.

Tile and Marble Setters (47-2044)

Tile and marble setters apply hard tile, marble, and wood tiles to walls, floors, ceilings, countertops, patios, and roof decks. Because tile and marble must be set on smooth, even surfaces, installers often must level the surface to be tiled with a layer of mortar or plywood.

3. ARTS, A/V TECHNOLOGY, AND COMMUNICATIONS

Workers in the performing arts, the visual arts, communications, and entertainment use a variety of media and venues to express ideas and emotions. Through the media of music, speech, and movement, performing artists may communicate a message or simply provide entertainment. In addition to the performing arts, athletic and sporting events provide entertainment and enjoyment to millions of viewers. The visual arts use visual means such as light, space, color, and texture to convey feelings or create a particular result. People in communications do research, writing, editing, and production. They use the written or spoken word to inform, persuade, or entertain others.

The following occupations are included in the Arts, A/V Technology and Communications Career Cluster. For further information about a specific occupation go to *www.bls.gov/ooh/* and key the name of the occupation in the search window.

Actors (27-2011)

Actors express ideas and portray characters in theater, film, television, and other performing arts media. They also work at theme parks or for other live events. They interpret a writer's script to entertain or inform an audience.

Announcers (27-3011, 3012)

Announcers present music, news, and sports and may provide commentary or interview guests about these topics or other important events. Some act as a master of ceremonies (emcee) or disc jockey (DJ) at weddings, parties, or clubs.

Art Directors (27-1011)

Art directors are responsible for the visual style and images in magazines, newspapers, product packaging, and movie and television productions. They create the overall design and direct others who develop artwork or layouts.

Athletes and Sports Competitors (27-2021)

Athletes and sports competitors participate in organized, officiated sports events to entertain spectators. However, few people who dream of becoming a paid professional athlete beat the odds and make a full-time living from professional athletics.

Broadcast and Sound Engineering Technicians (27-4011, 4012, 4014)

Broadcast and sound engineering technicians set up, operate, and maintain the electrical equipment for radio and television broadcasts, concerts, sound recordings, and movies and in office and school buildings.

Coaches and Scouts (27-2022)

Coaches teach amateur and professional athletes the skills they need to succeed at their sport. Scouts look for new players, evaluating athletes' strengths and weaknesses as possible recruits. Many coaches also scout out new talent.

Craft and Fine Artists (27-1012, 1013, 1019)

Craft and fine artists use a variety of materials and techniques to create art for sale and exhibition. Craft artists create handmade objects, such as pottery, glassware, textiles, or other objects that are designed to be functional. Fine artists, including painters, sculptors, and illustrators, create original works of art for their aesthetic value, rather than a functional one.

Dancers and Choreographers (27-2031, 2032)

Dancers and choreographers use movements to express ideas and stories in performances. There are many types of dance, such as

Part 2 Exploring Career Clusters

ballet, modern dance, tap, and jazz. Some people with dance backgrounds become dance teachers.

Editors (27-3041)

Editors plan, coordinate, and revise material for publication in books, newspapers, magazines, or websites. Editors review story ideas and decide what material will appeal most to readers. They also review and edit drafts of books and articles, offer comments to improve the product, and suggest titles and headlines.

Fashion Designers (27-1022)

Fashion designers create original clothing, accessories, and footwear. They sketch designs, select fabrics and patterns, and give instructions on how to make the products they designed. Some fashion designers specialize in clothing, footwear, or accessory design, but others create designs in all three fashion categories.

Film and Video Editors and Camera Operators (27-4030, 4031, 4032)

Film and video editors and camera operators record images that entertain or inform an audience. Camera operators capture a wide range of material for TV shows, motion pictures, music videos, documentaries, or news and sporting events. Editors construct the final productions from the many different images camera operators capture. They collaborate with producers and directors to create the final production.

Floral Designers (27-1023)

Floral designers, also called florists, cut and arrange live, dried, or silk flowers and greenery to make decorative displays. They also help customers select flowers, containers, ribbons, and other accessories. Floral designers may create a single arrangement for a special occasion or design floral displays for rooms and open spaces for large scale functions, such as weddings, funerals, and banquets.

Graphic Designers (27-1024)

Graphic designers create visual concepts, by hand or using computer software, to communicate ideas that inspire, inform, or captivate consumers. They help to make an organization recognizable by selecting color, images, or logo designs that represent a particular idea or identity to be used in advertising and promotions.

Industrial Designers (27-1021)

Industrial designers develop the concepts for manufactured products, such as cars, home appliances, and toys. They combine art, business, and engineering to make products that people use every day. Industrial designers generally focus on a particular product category. For example, some design medical equipment, while others work on consumer electronics products, such as computers or smart phones.

Interior Designers (27-1025)

Interior designers make interior spaces functional, safe, and beautiful for almost every type of building: offices, homes, airport terminals, shopping malls, and restaurants. They select and specify colors, finishes, fabrics, furniture, flooring and wall coverings, lighting, and other materials to create useful and stylish interiors for buildings.

Interpreters and Translators (27-3091)

Interpreters and translators aid communication by converting information from one language into another. Although some people do both, interpreting and translating are different professions: interpreters deal with spoken words, translators with written words.

Multimedia Artists and Animators (27-1014)

Multimedia artists and animators create animation and visual effects for television, movies, video games, and other media. They create two- and three-dimensional models and animation. Multimedia artists and animators often work in a specific medium.

Some focus on creating animated movies or video games. Others create visual effects for movies and television shows.

Music Directors and Composers (27-2041)

Music directors (also called conductors) lead orchestras and other musical groups during performances and recording sessions. Composers write and arrange original music in a variety of musical styles. Some music directors and composers work as self-enrichment teachers, giving private music lessons to children and adults.

Musicians and Singers (27-2042)

Musicians and singers play instruments or sing for live audiences and in recording studios. They perform in a variety of styles, such as classical, jazz, opera, rap, or rock. In some cases, musicians and singers write their own music to record and perform.

Photographers (27-4021)

Photographers use their technical expertise, creativity, and composition skills to produce and preserve images that visually tell a story or record an event. Today, most photographers use digital cameras instead of the traditional silver-halide film cameras. In addition, some photographers teach photography classes or conduct workshops in schools or in their own studios.

Reporters, Correspondents, and Broadcast News Analysts (27-3021, 3022)

Reporters, correspondents, and broadcast news analysts inform the public about news and events happening internationally, nationally, and locally. They report the news for newspapers, magazines, websites, television, and radio. They spend a lot of time in the field, conducting interviews and investigating stories. They travel to be on location for events or to meet contacts and file stories remotely.

Producers and Directors (27-2012)

Producers and directors are in charge of creating motion pictures, television shows, live theater, and other performing arts productions. They interpret a writer's script to entertain or inform an audience. **Producers** make the business and financial decisions for a motion picture, TV show, or stage production. **Directors** are responsible for the creative decisions of a production.

Set and Exhibit Designers (27-1027)

Set designers create sets for movie, television, theater, and other productions. They analyze scripts or other research documents to determine how many sets will be needed and how each set can best support the story. Exhibit designers create spaces to display products, art, or artifacts.

Technical Writers (27-3042)

Technical writers, also called technical communicators, produce instruction manuals and other supporting documents to communicate complex and technical information more easily. They also develop, gather, and disseminate technical information among customers, designers, and manufacturers.

Umpires, Referees, and Other Sports Officials (27-2023)

Umpires, referees, and other sports officials preside over competitive athletic or sporting events. They detect infractions and decide penalties according to the rules of the game. In officiating at sporting events, umpires, referees, and sports officials anticipate play and put themselves where they can best see the action, assess the situation, and determine any violations of the rules.

Writers and Authors (27-3043)

Writers and authors develop original written content for advertisements, books, magazines, movie and television scripts, songs, and online publications. An increasing number of writers are freelance writers—that is, they are self-employed and make their living by selling their written content to book and magazine publishers; news organizations; advertising agencies; and movie, theater, and television producers.

4. BUSINESS, MANAGEMENT, AND ADMINISTRATION

Managerial occupations involve an interest in planning, organizing, directing, and controlling the major functions of a business or organization. In a small business, a single owner-operator generally performs all management functions. However, as the size and complexity of an organization increase, so does the management hierarchy. Giant corporations contain several layers of management that are generally grouped into three levels. Top-level executives establish the objectives of the organization and chart its future course. Mid-level managers hold intermediary positions between supervisory and top management. Many of these managers are responsible for a specific activity such as personnel, finance, training and development, or public relations. Supervisory, or junior, managers plan, schedule, and supervise the day-to-day work of employees. Finally, most businesses have a large administrative support staff. Workers in this group prepare and keep records; operate office machines; arrange schedules and reservations; answer phones and greet visitors; prepare and account for correspondence and messages; or perform similar administrative duties.

The following occupations are included in the Business, Management and Administration Career Cluster. For further information about a specific occupation go to *www.bls.gov/ooh/* and key the name of the occupation in the search window.

Administrative Services Managers (11-3011)

Administrative services managers plan, direct, and coordinate supportive services of an organization. Their specific responsibilities vary by the type of organization and may include keeping records, distributing mail, and planning and maintaining facilities. In a small organization, they may direct all support services and may be called the business office manager.

Compensation and Benefits Managers (11-3111)

Compensation managers plan, direct, and coordinate how and how much an organization pays its employees. Benefits managers do the same for retirement plans, health insurance, and other benefits an organization offers its employees.

Financial Managers (11-3031)

Financial managers are responsible for the financial health of an organization. They produce financial reports, direct investment activities, and develop strategies and plans for the long-term financial goals of their organization.

General Office Clerks (43-9061)

General office clerks do a broad range of administrative tasks, including answering telephones, typing or word processing, and filing. However, tasks vary widely in different jobs. Rather than doing a single specialized task, general office clerks have responsibilities that often change daily with the needs of the specific job and the employer.

Human Resources Managers (11-3121)

Human resources managers plan, direct, and coordinate the administrative functions of an organization. They oversee the recruiting, interviewing, and hiring of new staff; consult with top executives on strategic planning; and serve as a link between an organization's management and its employees.

Human Resources Specialists (13-1078)

Human resources specialists recruit, screen, interview, and place workers. They also may handle human resources work in a variety of other areas, such as employee relations, payroll and benefits, and training. Many specialists are trained in all human resources disciplines and do tasks throughout all areas of the HR department.

Information Clerks (43-4000)

Information clerks provide administrative and clerical support in a variety of settings. They help maintain records, collect data and information, and respond to customers' questions or concerns. Information clerks generally manage a particular kind of information or record, such as file clerks, correspondence clerks, court clerks, or license clerks.

Management Analysts (13-1111)

Management analysts, often called management consultants, propose ways to improve an organization's efficiency. They advise managers on how to make organizations more profitable through reduced costs and increased revenues. Although some management analysts work for the organization that they are analyzing, most work as consultants on a contractual basis.

Public Relations Managers and Specialists (11- 3031)

Public relations managers and specialists create and maintain a favorable public image for their employer or client. They write material for media releases, plan and direct public relations programs, and raise funds for their organization.

Receptionists (43-4171)

Receptionists perform various administrative tasks, including answering telephones and giving information to the public and customers. Receptionists are often the first employee that the public or customer has contact with. They are responsible for making a good first impression for the organization, which can affect the organization's success.

Secretaries and Administrative Assistants (43-6000)

Secretaries and administrative assistants perform a variety of clerical and organizational tasks that are necessary to run an organization efficiently. They organize files, draft messages, schedule appointments, and support other staff. Specific job duties vary by experience, job title, and specialty.

Top Executives (11-1011, 1021)

Top executives devise strategies and policies to ensure that an organization meets its goals. They plan, direct, and coordinate operational activities of companies and public or private-sector organizations. The responsibilities of top executives largely depend on an organization's size.

Training and Development Managers (11-3131)

Training and development managers plan, direct, and coordinate programs to enhance the knowledge and skills of an organization's employees. They also oversee a staff of training and development specialists. Training and development managers work to align training and development with an organization's goals.

Part 2 Exploring Career Clusters

5. EDUCATION AND TRAINING

This cluster includes occupations in teaching, educational administration, counseling, and library science. Teachers help students gain the knowledge and skills needed to function in the world. Educational administrators manage schools and colleges and supervise the faculty and support staff. Counselors provide personal, social, and career guidance in a wide range of settings. Librarians manage libraries and learning centers. They assist individuals with information needs ranging from recreational reading to specialized research. Archivists and curators also help people learn and gain information, but they work primarily with objects such as historical documents.

The following occupations are included in the Education and Training Career Cluster. For further information about a specific occupation go to *www.bls.gov/ooh/* and key the name of the occupation in the search window.

Adult Literacy and GED Teachers (25-3011)

Adult literacy and General Education Development (GED) teachers instruct adults and youths who are out of school in basic skills, such as reading, writing, and speaking English. They also help students earn their GED or high school diploma.

Archivists (25-4011)

Archivists appraise, edit, and maintain permanent records and historically valuable documents. Many perform research on archival material. They also preserve many documents and records for their importance, potential value, or historical significance. Most archivists coordinate educational and public outreach programs, such as tours, workshops, lectures, and classes.

Career and Technical Education Teachers (25-2023, 2032)

Career and technical education teachers help students in middle school and high school develop career-related and technical skills. They help students explore or prepare to enter a particular occupation, such as one in auto repair, healthcare, business, or the culinary arts.

Curators, Museum Technicians, and Conservators (25-4012, 4013)

Curators oversee collections, such as artwork and historic items, and may conduct public service activities for an institution. Museum technicians and conservators prepare and restore objects and documents in museum collections and exhibits.

Elementary, Middle, and High School Principals (11-9032)

Elementary, middle, and high school principals lead teachers and other members of school staff. They manage the day-to-day operations of elementary, middle, and high schools. They set goals and objectives and evaluate their school's progress toward meeting them.

High School Teachers (25-2031)

High school teachers help prepare students for life after graduation. They teach academic lessons and various skills that students will need to attend college and to enter the job market. High school teachers generally teach students from the 9th through 12th grades. They usually teach one or two of the subjects (such as history, math or English) or classes a student has throughout the day.

Instructional Coordinators (25-9031)

Instructional coordinators oversee school districts' curriculums and teaching standards. They work with teachers and school administrators to implement new teaching techniques to improve the quality of education. They make changes to the curriculum and adopt new teaching strategies and techniques to improve students' test scores and outcomes.

Kindergarten and Elementary School Teachers (25-2012, 2021)

Kindergarten and elementary school teachers prepare younger students for future schooling by teaching them the basics of subjects such as math and reading. Kindergarten and elementary school teachers act as facilitators or coaches to help students learn and apply important concepts. Many teachers use a hands-on approach, including props, to help students understand abstract concepts, solve problems, and develop critical thinking skills.

Librarians (25-4021)

Librarians help people find information from many sources. They maintain library collections and do other work as needed to keep the library running. Librarians who work in different settings (such as law firms, government agencies, and medical schools) often have different job duties.

Library Technicians and Assistants (25-4031, 4121)

Library technicians and assistants help librarians acquire, prepare, and organize materials. They also do other tasks that are needed to run a library. Library technicians and assistants are usually supervised by a librarian. Library technicians may have more responsibilities than library assistants, such as administering library programs and overseeing lower-level staff.

Middle School Teachers (25-2022)

Middle school teachers educate students, most of whom are in sixth through eighth grades. They help students build on the fundamentals they learned in elementary school and prepare them for the more difficult lessons they will learn in high school.

Postsecondary Education Administrators (11-9033)

Postsecondary education administrators oversee student services, academics, and research at colleges and universities. Their job duties vary depending on the area of the college they manage, such as admissions, student life, or the office of the registrar.

Postsecondary Teachers (25-1000)

Postsecondary teachers instruct students in a wide variety of academic and vocational subjects beyond the high school level. They also conduct research and publish scholarly papers and books. Professors and other postsecondary teachers specialize in any of a wide variety of subjects and fields. Some teach academic subjects, such as English or philosophy. Others focus on career-related subjects, such as law, nursing, or culinary arts.

Preschool and Childcare Center Directors (11-9031)

Preschool and childcare center directors are responsible for all aspects of their program. They direct and lead staff, oversee daily activities, and prepare plans and budgets. Some preschools and childcare centers are independently owned and operated. Other preschools and childcare centers are part of a national chain or franchise.

Preschool Teachers (25-2011)

Preschool teachers educate and care for children, usually ages 3 to 5, who have not yet entered kindergarten. They explain reading, writing, science, and other subjects in a way that young children can understand. Preschool teachers often use play to teach children about the world. For example, they use storytelling and rhyming games to teach language and vocabulary.

School and Career Counselors (21-1012)

School counselors help students develop social skills and succeed in school. Career counselors assist people with the process of making career decisions by helping them choose a career or educational program. The

Part 2 Exploring Career Clusters

specific duties of school counselors vary with the ages of the students they work with.

Self-enrichment Teachers (25-3021)

Self-enrichment teachers instruct in a variety of subjects that students take for fun or self-improvement, such as music and foreign languages. These classes generally do not lead to a degree or certification, and students take them voluntarily to learn new skills or gain understanding of a subject.

Special Education Teachers (25-2041, 2053, 2054)

Special education teachers work with students who have a wide range of learning, mental, emotional and physical disabilities. With students who have mild or moderate disabilities, they ensure that lessons and teaching strategies are modified to meet the students' needs. With students who have severe disabilities, they teach the students independent living skills and basic literacy, communication, and math.

Teacher Assistants (25-9041)

Teacher assistants provide instructional and clerical support for classroom teachers. They work under a teacher's supervision to give students additional attention and instruction. Teacher assistants are also called teacher aides, instructional aides, paraprofessionals, and paraeducators. Some teacher assistants work only with special education students who may need additional attention.

6. FINANCE

This cluster includes occupations in banking, business financial management, financial planning, and insurance. Finance occupations are available in every sector of the economy and employ millions of people. Banking services is the largest group, which is available through commercial banks, mutual savings banks, savings and loan associations, and credit unions. Banking services are primarily concerned with accepting customer deposits, making loans, and providing credit. Insurance services is another large group of financial occupations that exists to protect individuals and businesses from financial losses and to provide services in the event of a catastrophe. Financial planners help individuals and business to invest for the future. They also serve as intermediaries in the purchase of stocks, bonds, and other investments. Financial managers are responsible for financial operations in a wide variety of businesses and organizations. Large numbers of support personnel including financial clerks, tellers, and account collectors aid the work of financial professionals.

The following occupations are included in the Finance Career Cluster. For further information about a specific occupation go to *www.bls.gov/ooh/* and key the name of the occupation in the search window.

Accountants and Auditors (13-2011)

Accountants and auditors prepare and examine financial records. They ensure that financial records are accurate and that taxes are paid properly and on time. Accountants and auditors assess financial operations and work to help ensure that organizations run efficiently.

Appraisers and Assessors of Real Estate (13-2021)

Appraisers and assessors of real estate estimate the value of real property—land and the buildings on that land—before it is sold, mortgaged, taxed, insured, or developed. Appraisers and assessors work in localities that they are familiar with so that they know any environmental or other concerns that may affect the property's value.

Bill and Account Collectors (43-3011)

Bill and account collectors, sometimes called collectors, try to recover payment on overdue bills. They negotiate repayment plans with debtors and help them find solutions to make paying their overdue bills easier. Bill and account collectors generally contact debtors by phone, although sometimes they do so by mail. They use computer systems to update contact information and record past collection attempts with a particular debtor.

Bookkeeping, Accounting, and Auditing Clerks (43-3031)

Bookkeeping, accounting, and auditing clerks produce financial records for organizations. They record financial transactions, update statements, and check financial records for accuracy. The records they work with include expenditures (money spent), receipts (money that comes in), accounts payable (bills to be paid), accounts receivable (invoices, or what other people owe the organization), and profit and loss (a report that shows the organization's financial health).

Budget Analysts (13-2031)

Budget analysts help public and private institutions organize their finances. They prepare budget reports and monitor institutional spending. They prepare annual and special reports and evaluate budget

Part 2 Exploring Career Clusters

proposals. They analyze data to determine the costs and benefits of various programs and recommend funding levels based on their findings.

Claims Adjusters, Appraisers, Examiners, and Investigators (13-1030)

Claims adjusters, appraisers, examiners, and investigators evaluate insurance claims. They decide whether an insurance company must pay a claim, and if so, how much. What insurance adjusters, examiners, and investigators do varies by the type of insurance company they work for. They must know a lot about what their company insures.

Cost Estimators (13-1051)

Cost estimators collect and analyze data to estimate the time, money, resources, and labor required for product manufacturing, construction projects, or services. Accurately predicting the cost, size, and duration of future construction and manufacturing projects is vital to the survival of any business. Cost estimators' calculations give managers or investors this information.

Financial Analysts (13-2051)

Financial analysts provide guidance to businesses and individuals making investment decisions. They assess the performance of stocks, bonds, and other types of investments. They work in banks, pension funds, mutual funds, securities firms, insurance companies, and other businesses. They are also called securities analysts and investment analysts.

Financial Clerks (43-3000)

Financial clerks give administrative and clerical support in financial settings. They do administrative work for banking, insurance, and other companies. They keep records, help customers, and carry out financial transactions.

Financial Examiners (13-2061)

Financial examiners ensure compliance with laws governing financial institutions and transactions. They typically work in one of two main areas: risk scoping or consumer compliance. Those working in risk scoping evaluate the health of financial institutions. Financial examiners working in consumer compliance monitor lending activity to ensure that borrowers are treated fairly.

Financial Managers (11-3031)

Financial managers are responsible for the financial health of an organization. They produce financial reports, direct investment activities, and develop strategies and plans for the long-term financial goals of their organization. Their main responsibility used to be monitoring a company's finances, but they now do more data analysis and advise senior managers on ideas to maximize profits.

Insurance Underwriters (13-2053)

Insurance underwriters decide whether to provide insurance and under what terms. They evaluate insurance applications and determine coverage amounts and premiums. Insurance underwriters must achieve a balance between risky and cautious decisions. If underwriters allow too much risk, the insurance company will pay out too many claims. However, if they do not approve enough applications, the company will not make enough money from premiums.

Loan Officers (13-2072)

Loan officers evaluate, authorize, or recommend approval of loan applications for people and businesses. They use a process called underwriting to assess whether applicants qualify for loans. After collecting and verifying all the required financial documents, the loan officer evaluates this information to determine the applicant's loan needs and ability to pay back the loan.

Personal Financial Advisors (13-2052)

Personal financial advisors assess the financial needs of individuals and help them with investments (such as stocks and bonds), tax laws, and insurance decisions.

Advisors help clients plan for short-term and long-term goals, such as education expenses and retirement. They recommend investments to match the clients' goals. They invest clients' money based on the clients' decisions.

Property, Real Estate, and Community Association Managers (11-9141)

Property, real estate, and community association managers take care of the many aspects of residential, commercial, or industrial properties. They make sure the property looks nice, operates smoothly, and preserves its resale value. Handling the financial operations of the property is an important part of what they do.

Securities, Commodities, and Financial Services Sales Agents (41-3031)

Securities, commodities, and financial services sales agents connect buyers and sellers in financial markets. They sell securities to individuals, advise companies in search of investors, and conduct trades. Agents spend much of the day interacting with people, whether selling stock to an individual or discussing the status of a merger deal with a company executive.

Tellers (43-3071)

Tellers are responsible for accurately processing routine transactions at a bank. These transactions include cashing checks, depositing money, and collecting loan payments. Tellers also seek out customers who might want to buy more financial products or services from the bank, such as certificates of deposits (CDs) and loans.

Part 2 Exploring Career Clusters

7. GOVERNMENT AND PUBLIC ADMINISTRATION

Virtually every occupation can be found within this cluster. However, some activities and occupations are unique to government. Government workers include elected or appointed public officials responsible for making and executing public policy. Members of our armed forces serve throughout the world to protect and defend the national security. Planning workers develop policies for land use, promote the wise use of a community's resources, and provide data for local officials to make informed decisions. Revenue and taxation workers collect tax dollars, review tax returns, conduct audits, and collect overdue tax dollars. Regulation workers help protect health, safety, and the environment through audits, inspections, and investigations required to enforce various laws and regulations. And, of course, postal workers collect, sort, and deliver the mail.

The following occupations are included in the Government and Public Administration Career Cluster. For further information about a specific occupation go to *www.bls.gov/ooh/* and key the name of the occupation in the search window.

Atmospheric Scientists, Including Meteorologists (19-2021)

Atmospheric scientists study weather, climate, and other aspects of the atmosphere. They develop reports and forecasts from their analysis of weather and climate data. Atmospheric scientists use highly developed instruments and computer programs to do their jobs. The data they collect and analyze are critical to understanding air pollution, drought, loss of the ozone layer, and other problems.

Cartographers and Photogrammetrists (17-1021)

Cartographers and photogrammetrists measure, analyze, and interpret geographic information to create maps and charts for political, cultural, educational, and other purposes. Cartographers are general mapmakers, and photogrammetrists are specialized mapmakers who use aerial photographs to create maps.

Economists (19-3011)

Economists study the production and distribution of resources, goods, and services. They apply economic analysis to issues within a variety of fields, such as education, health, development, and the environment. Some economists study the cost of products, healthcare, or energy. Others examine employment levels, business cycles, or exchange rates. Still others analyze the effect of taxes, inflation, or interest rates.

Epidemiologists (19-1041)

Epidemiologists investigate the causes of disease and other public health problems to prevent them from spreading or from happening again. They report their findings to public policy officials and to the general public. Research epidemiologists typically work for universities. Applied epidemiologists work with governments, addressing health crises directly. The most common problem both types of epidemiologists work on is infectious diseases.

Geographers (19-3092)

Geographers study the earth and its land, features, and inhabitants. They also examine phenomena such as political or cultural structures as they relate to geography. They study the physical or human geographic characteristics or both of a region, ranging in scale from local to global.

Historians

Historians conduct research and analysis for governments, businesses, nonprofits, historical associations, and other organizations. They use a variety of sources in their work, including government and institutional records, newspapers, photographs, interviews, films, and unpublished manuscripts such as personal diaries and letters. They also may process, catalog, and archive these documents and artifacts.

Legislators (11-1031)

Legislators are elected officials who develop laws for the federal government, or for local or state governments. Legislators are members of the legislative branch of government, which is responsible for making new laws and changing existing laws. Legislators include members of the U.S. Congress; state senators and representatives; and city, county, and township commissioners and council members.

Military

The U.S. Military provides training and work experience in a variety of military occupations. Members of the Armed Forces work in almost all occupations that are available to civilians in addition to occupations that are specific to the military. Service men and women serve on active duty in the Army, Navy, Air Force, and Marine Corps, or in the Reserve components of these branches, and the Air National Guard and Army National Guard. (The Coast Guard, which is included in this profile, is part of the Department of Homeland Security.)

Police, Fire, and Ambulance Dispatchers (43-5031)

Police, fire, and ambulance dispatchers, also called 9-1-1 operators or public safety telecommunicators, answer emergency and non-emergency calls. They take information from the caller and send the appropriate type and number of units. Dispatchers answer calls for service when someone needs help from police, fire fighters, emergency services, or a combination of the three.

Political Scientists (19-3094)

Political scientists study the origin, development, and operation of political systems. They research political ideas and analyze the structure and operation of governments, policies, political trends, and related issues. Political scientists usually conduct research within one of four primary subfields: American politics, comparative politics, international relations, or political theory.

Postal Service Workers (43-5050)

Postal Service workers sell postal products and collect, sort, and deliver mail. Postal Service workers receive and process mail for delivery to homes, businesses, and post office boxes. Workers are classified based on the type of work they perform.

Social and Community Service Managers (11-9151)

Social and community service managers coordinate and supervise social service programs and community organizations that provide services to the public. They work for nonprofit organizations, private for-profit social service companies, and government agencies. Some managers focus on working with a particular population, such as children, homeless people, or veterans; others focus on helping people with particular challenges, such as hunger or joblessness.

Sociologists (19-3041)

Sociologists study human social lives, activities, interactions, processes, and organizations within the context of larger social, political, and economic forces. They examine how social influences affect different individuals and groups, and the ways organizations and institutions affect people's lives.

Survey Researchers (19-3022)

Survey researchers design or conduct surveys and analyze survey data. Many groups use surveys to collect factual data, such as employment and salary information, or to ask questions that help them understand people's opinions, attitudes, beliefs, or desires.

Tax Examiners and Collectors, and Revenue Agents (13-2081)

Different levels of government collect different types of taxes. The federal government deals primarily with personal and business income taxes. State governments collect income and sales taxes. Local governments collect sales and property taxes. Tax examiners and collectors, and revenue agents ensure that governments get their tax money from businesses and citizens. They review tax returns, conduct audits, identify taxes owed, and collect overdue tax payments.

Urban and Regional Planners (19-3051)

Urban and regional planners develop plans and programs for the use of land. They use planning to create communities, accommodate growth, or revitalize physical facilities in towns, cities, counties, and metropolitan areas. They identify community needs and develop short- and long-term plans to create, grow, or revitalize a community or area. For example, planners may examine plans for proposed facilities, such as schools, to ensure that these facilities will meet the needs of a changing population.

8. HEALTH SCIENCE

This cluster includes three major groups of occupations: health diagnosing practitioners; health assessment and treating occupations; and health technologists, technicians, assistants, and aides. Health practitioners (such as physicians, optometrists, dentists, and veterinarians) diagnose, treat, and strive to prevent illness and disease. While all of them practice the art of healing, they differ in methods of treatment and areas of specialization. Health assessment and treating workers care for the sick, help the disabled, and advise individuals and communities on ways of maintaining and improving their health. Nursing is by far the largest of these occupations. Most occupations in the third group (such as dental hygienists, emergency medical technicians, surgical technicians, and aides) are designed to extend the services of highly skilled health practitioners. Many occupations is this group owe their existence to the development of new laboratory procedures, diagnostic techniques, and treatment methods. Quite a few of these involve clinical applications of the computer and operating or monitoring biomedical equipment.

The following occupations are included in the Health Science Career Cluster. For further information about a specific occupation go to *www.bls.gov/ooh/* and key the name of the occupation in the search window.

Athletic Trainers (29-9091)

Athletic trainers specialize in preventing, diagnosing, and treating muscle and bone injuries and illnesses. They work with people of all ages and all skill levels, from young children to soldiers and professional athletes. Athletic trainers must be able to recognize, evaluate, and assess injuries and provide immediate care when needed.

Audiologists (29-1181)

Audiologists work with people who have hearing, balance and related ear problems. They examine individuals of all ages and identify those with the symptoms of hearing loss and other auditory, balance, and related sensory and neural problems. Audiologists then assess the nature and extent of the problems and help individuals manage them.

Cardiovascular Technologists and Technicians and Vascular Technologists (29-2031)

Cardiovascular technologists and technicians and vascular technologists use imaging technology to help physicians diagnose cardiac (heart) and peripheral vascular (blood vessel) ailments in patients. They also help physicians treat problems with cardiac and vascular systems, such as blood clots.

Chiropractors (29-1011)

Chiropractors treat patients with health problems of the musculoskeletal system, which is made up of bones, muscles, ligaments, and tendons. They use spinal manipulation and other techniques to treat patients' ailments, such as back or neck pain.

Dental Assistants (31-9091)

Dental assistants have many tasks, ranging from patient care to record keeping, in a dental office. They work at chair-side as dentists examine and treat patients. Their duties vary by state and by the dentists' offices where they work.

Dental Hygienists (29-2021)

Dental hygienists clean teeth, examine patients for oral diseases such as gingivitis, and provide other preventative dental care. In some states, dental hygienists place

temporary fillings and dressings; remove
sutures; and smooth and polish metal
restorations such as fillings and crowns.
They also educate patients on ways to
improve and maintain good oral health.

Dentists (29-1020)

Dentists diagnose and treat problems with a
patient's teeth, gums, and other parts of the
mouth. They remove teeth, fill cavities,
straighten and repair teeth, and treat gum
diseases. Dentists provide advice and
instruction on taking care of teeth and gums
and on diet choices that affect oral health.

Diagnostic Medical Sonographers (29-2032)

Diagnostic medical sonographers use special
imaging equipment that directs sound waves
into a patient's body (in a procedure
commonly known as an ultrasound,
sonogram, or echocardiogram) to assess and
diagnose various medical conditions.

Dietitians and Nutritionists (29-1031)

Dietitians and nutritionists are experts in
food and nutrition. They plan nutrition
programs and supervise the preparation and
serving of meals. They advise people on what
to eat in order to lead a healthy lifestyle or
achieve a specific health-related goal.

EMTs and Paramedics (29-2041)

Emergency medical technicians (EMTs) and
paramedics care for the sick or injured in
emergency medical settings. People's lives
often depend on their quick reaction and
competent care. EMTs and paramedics
respond to emergency calls, performing
medical services and transporting patients
to medical facilities.

Health Educators (21-1091)

Health educators teach people about
behaviors that promote wellness. They
develop programs and materials to encourage
people to make healthy decisions. The duties
of health educators vary based on where they
work. Most work in health care facilities,
colleges, public health departments,
nonprofits, and private businesses.

Home Health and Personal Care Aides (31-1011, 39-9021)

Home health and personal care aides help
people who are disabled, chronically ill, or
cognitively impaired. They also help older
adults who may need assistance. They help
with activities such as bathing and dressing,
and they provide services such as light
housekeeping. In some states, home health
aides may be able to give a client medication
or check the client's vital signs under the
direction of a nurse or other healthcare
practitioner.

Licensed Practical and Licensed Vocational Nurses (29-2061)

Licensed practical and licensed vocational
nurses (known as LPNs or LVNs, depending
on the state in which they work) provide
basic nursing care. They take vital signs,
give injections, apply dressings, help with
bathing and dressing, and care for emotional
needs. They work under the direction of
registered nurses and doctors.

Massage Therapists (31-9011)

Massage therapists treat clients by using
touch to manipulate the soft-tissue muscles
of the body. With their touch, therapists
relieve pain, rehabilitate injuries, reduce
stress, increase relaxation, and aid in the
general wellness of clients.

Medical and Clinical Laboratory Technologists and Technicians (29-2011, 29-2012)

Medical laboratory technologists (also
known as medical laboratory scientists) and
medical laboratory technicians collect
samples and perform tests to analyze body
fluids, tissue, and other substances. Both
technicians and technologists perform tests
and procedures that physicians or other
healthcare personnel order. However,
technologists perform more complex tests and
laboratory procedures than technicians do.

Medical Assistants (31-9092)

Medical assistants complete administrative
and clinical tasks in the offices of physicians,

podiatrists, chiropractors, and other health practitioners. Their duties vary with the location, specialty, and size of the practice. In some states, tasks may include helping physicians examine and treat patients.

Medical and Health Services Managers (11-9111)

Medical and health services managers, also called healthcare executives or healthcare administrators, plan, direct, and coordinate medical and health services. They might manage an entire facility, specialize in managing a specific clinical area or department, or manage a medical practice for a group of physicians.

Medical Records and Health Information Technicians (29-2071)

Medical records and health information technicians organize and manage health information data by ensuring its quality, accuracy, accessibility, and security in both paper and electronic systems. They use various classification systems to code and categorize patient information for reimbursement purposes, for databases and registries, and to maintain patients' medical and treatment histories.

Medical Scientists (19-1042)

Medical scientists study biological systems to understand the causes of diseases and other health problems. They conduct research aimed at improving overall human health. They often use clinical trials and other investigative methods to reach their findings.

Medical Transcriptionists (31-9094)

Medical transcriptionists listen to voice recordings that physicians and other health professionals make and convert them into written reports. They interpret medical terminology and abbreviations in preparing patients' medical histories, discharge summaries, and other documents.

Nuclear Medicine Technologists (29-2033)

Nuclear medicine technologists use a scanner to create images of various areas of a patient's body. They prepare radioactive drugs and administer them to patients undergoing the scans. The radioactive drugs cause abnormal areas of the body to appear different from normal areas in the images.

Nursing Aides, Orderlies, and Attendants (31-1012)

Nursing aides, orderlies, and attendants help provide basic care for patients in hospitals and residents of long-term care facilities, such as nursing homes. Some nursing aides and attendants may also dispense medication, depending on their training level and the state in which they work.

Occupational Health and Safety Specialists (29-9011)

Occupational health and safety specialists analyze many types of work environments and work procedures. Specialists inspect workplaces for adherence to regulations on safety, health, and the environment. They also design programs to prevent disease or injury to workers and damage to the environment.

Occupational Health and Safety Technicians (29-9012)

Occupational health and safety technicians collect data on the safety and health conditions of the workplace. Technicians work with occupational health and safety specialists in conducting tests and measuring hazards to help prevent harm to workers, property, the environment, and the general public.

Occupational Therapists (29-1122)

Occupational therapists treat patients with injuries, illnesses, or disabilities through the therapeutic use of everyday activities. They help these patients develop, recover, and improve the skills needed for daily living and working.

Occupational Therapy Assistants and Aides (31-2011, 2012)

Occupational therapy assistants and aides work under the direction of occupational therapists in treating patients with injuries, illnesses, or disabilities through the therapeutic use of everyday activities. They help these patients develop, recover, and improve the skills needed for daily living and working.

Opticians, Dispensing (29-2081)

Dispensing opticians help fit eyeglasses and contact lenses, following prescriptions from ophthalmologists and optometrists. They also help customers decide which eyeglass frames or type of contact lenses to buy.

Optometrists (29-1041)

Optometrists perform eye exams to check for vision problems and diseases. They prescribe eyeglasses or contact lenses as needed. Many optometrists own their practice and may also spend time on general business activities such as hiring employees and ordering supplies.

Orthotists and Prosthetists (29-2091)

Orthotists and prosthetists, also called O&P professionals, design medical support devices and measure and fit patients for them. These devices include artificial limbs (arms, hands, legs, and feet), braces, and other medical or surgical devices.

Pharmacists (29-1051)

Pharmacists dispense prescription medications to patients and offer advice on their safe use. With most drugs, pharmacists use standard dosages from pharmaceutical companies. However, some pharmacists create customized medications by mixing ingredients themselves, a process known as compounding.

Pharmacy Technicians (29-2052)

Pharmacy technicians help licensed pharmacists dispense prescription medication. They work under the supervision of pharmacists, who must review all prescriptions before they are given to patients. They work in retail pharmacies and hospitals.

Physical Therapist Assistants and Aides (31-2021, 2022)

Physical therapist assistants and physical therapist aides work under the direction of physical therapists. They help patients who are recovering from injuries, illnesses, and surgeries regain movement and manage pain.

Physical Therapists (29-1123)

Physical therapists help people who have injuries or illnesses improve their movement and manage their pain. They are often an important part of rehabilitation and treatment of patients with chronic conditions or injuries.

Physician Assistants (29-1071)

Physician assistants, also known as PAs, practice medicine under the direction of physicians and surgeons. They are formally trained to examine patients, diagnose injuries and illnesses, and provide treatment.

Physicians and Surgeons (29-1060)

Physicians and surgeons diagnose and treat injuries and illnesses in patients. Physicians examine patients, take medical histories, prescribe medications, and order, perform, and interpret diagnostic tests. Surgeons operate on patients to treat injuries, such as broken bones; diseases, such as cancerous tumors; and deformities, such as cleft palates.

Podiatrists (29-1081)

Podiatrists provide medical and surgical care for people suffering foot, ankle, and lower leg problems. They diagnose illnesses, treat injuries, and perform surgery. They also fit corrective inserts called orthotics and design custom-made shoes.

Psychiatric Technicians and Aides
(29-2053, 31-1013)

Psychiatric technicians and aides care for people who have mental illness and developmental disabilities. The two occupations are related, but technicians typically provide therapeutic care, and aides help patients in their daily activities and ensure a safe, clean environment.

Radiation Therapists (29-1124)

Radiation therapists use machines to administer radiation treatments, primarily to cancer patients. They develop a treatment plan to meet the patients need in conjunction with a radiation oncologist (physician) and a dosimetrist (technician) who calculated the dose of radiation used for treatment.

Radiologic Technologists (29-2037)

Radiologic technologists perform diagnostic imaging examinations, such as x rays, on patients. They may be called CT technicians or MRI technicians, depending on the equipment they work with. Radiologic technologists might also specialize in mammography.

Recreational Therapists (29-1125)

Recreational therapists plan, direct, and coordinate recreation programs for people with disabilities or illnesses. They use a variety of techniques, including arts and crafts, drama, music, dance, sports, games, and field trips. These programs help maintain or improve a client's physical and emotional well-being.

Registered Nurses (29-1111)

Registered nurses (RNs) provide and coordinate patient care, educate patients and the public about various health conditions, and provide advice and emotional support to patients and their family members. State laws govern the specific tasks RNs may perform.

Respiratory Therapists (29-1126)

Respiratory therapists care for patients who have trouble breathing; for example, from a chronic respiratory disease, such as asthma or emphysema. They also provide emergency care to patients suffering from heart attacks, stroke, drowning, or shock.

Speech-Language Pathologists (29-1127)

Speech-language pathologists diagnose and treat communication and swallowing disorders in patients. They use a variety of treatment tools, including audiovisual equipment and computers.

Surgical Technologists (29-2955)

Surgical technologists, also called operating room technicians, assist in surgical operations. They prepare operating rooms, arrange equipment, and help doctors and nurses during surgeries.

Veterinarians (29-1131)

Veterinarians care for the health of animals. They diagnose, treat, or research medical conditions and diseases of pets, livestock, and animals in zoos, racetracks, and laboratories. The majority of veterinarians treat small companion animals such as dogs and cats.

Veterinary Assistants and Laboratory Animal Caretakers (31-9096)

Veterinary assistants and laboratory animal caretakers look after nonfarm animals in laboratories, animal hospitals, and clinics. They care for the well-being of animals by doing routine tasks under the supervision of veterinarians, scientists, or veterinary technologists or technicians.

Veterinary Technologists and Technicians (31-9096)

Veterinary technologists and technicians perform medical tests, nursing, and postoperative care under the supervision of a licensed veterinarian to treat or to help veterinarians diagnose the illnesses and injuries of animals. Despite differences in formal education and training, veterinary technologists and technicians carry out many similar tasks.

9. HOSPITALITY AND TOURISM

Hospitality and tourism occupations are unique in providing services for the convenience and enjoyment of others. Eating in a restaurant, going on a family vacation, visiting an amusement park, or being able to rest and relax as a part of business travel makes life easier and more pleasant for people. The largest group of hospitality and tourism occupations is food service workers. These workers plan, prepare, and serve food and beverages at all types of eating and drinking establishments. Lodging workers perform jobs related to the operation of lodging facilities and the care of guests who use these facilities. Food services and lodging are also an important part of the travel and tourism group of occupations. Travel and tourism workers provide services for both business and non-business travelers as well as for groups and organizations (for example, meetings and conventions). Recreation, amusement and attraction workers may provide short-term experiences, such as a day at the zoo or theme park, or be part of an extended family vacation. Workers in this career cluster may be found in all different aspects of hospitality and tourism. Hospitality and tourism services are supported by large numbers of entry-level workers such as bus persons, housekeeping cleaners, dishwashers, and gaming workers.

The following occupations are included in the Hospitality and Tourism Career Cluster. For further information about a specific occupation go to *www.bls.gov/ooh/* and key the name of the occupation in the search window.

Bartenders (35-3011)

Bartenders fill drink orders either directly from patrons at the bar or through waiters and waitresses who place drink orders for dining room customers. They must know a wide range of drink recipes and be able to mix drinks accurately, quickly, and without waste. Bartenders also are responsible for checking the identification of customers seated at the bar to ensure they meet the minimum age requirement.

Chefs and Head Cooks (35-1011)

Chefs and head cooks oversee the daily food preparation at restaurants or other places where food is served. They direct kitchen staff and handle any food-related concerns. Some chefs use scheduling and purchasing software to help them in their administrative duties.

Cooks (35-2010)

Cooks prepare, season, and cook a wide range of foods, such as soups, salads, entrees, and desserts. Cooks usually work under the direction or supervision of chefs, head cooks, or food service managers. The responsibilities of cooks vary depending on where they work, the size of the facility, and the complexity and level of service offered.

Food and Beverage Serving and Related Workers (35-3000)

Food and beverage serving and related workers are the front line of customer service in full-service restaurants, casual dining eateries, and other food service establishments. Depending on the establishment, they might take customers' food and drink orders and prepare and serve food and beverages. Most work as part of a team, helping coworkers to improve workflow and customer service.

Food Preparation Workers (35-2021)

Food preparation workers perform many routine tasks under the guidance of cooks or food supervisors. They prepare cold foods, slice meat, peel and cut vegetables, brew coffee or tea, and do many other tasks. Although most help prepare food, some are also responsible for retrieving cooking utensils, pots, and pans, or for cleaning and storing other kitchen equipment. Other common duties include keeping salad bars and buffet tables stocked and clean.

Food Service Managers (11-9051)

Food service managers are responsible for the daily operations of restaurants and other establishments that prepare and serve food and beverages to customers. Besides coordinating activities between the kitchen and dining room staff, managers must ensure that customers are served properly and in a timely manner. They monitor orders in the kitchen and, if needed, they work with the chef to remedy any delays in service.

Gaming Services Occupations (39-3010)

Gaming services workers serve customers in gambling establishments, such as casinos or racetracks. Some workers tend slot machines or deal cards. Others take bets or pay out winnings. Still others supervise gaming workers and operations.

Lodging Managers (11-9081)

A comfortable room, good food, and a helpful staff can make being away from home an enjoyable experience for guests on vacation or business travel. Lodging managers make sure that guests have a pleasant experience, while also ensuring that an establishment is run efficiently and profitably.

Maids and Housekeeping Cleaners (37-2012)

Maids and housekeeping cleaners do general cleaning tasks, including making beds and vacuuming halls, in private homes and commercial establishments. Those who work in hotels, hospitals, and other commercial establishments may also share other duties. For example, housekeeping cleaners in hotels may deliver ironing boards, cribs, and rollaway beds to guests' rooms.

Meeting, Convention, and Event Planners (13-1121)

Meeting, convention, and event planners coordinate all aspects of professional meetings and events. They choose meeting locations, arrange transportation, and coordinate other details. During the meeting, they handle meeting logistics such as registering guests and setting up audio/visual equipment for speakers. After the meeting, they survey attendees to find out what topics interested them the most.

Recreation Workers (39-9032)

Recreation workers design and lead leisure activities for groups in volunteer agencies or recreation facilities, such as playgrounds, parks, camps and senior centers. They may lead activities in areas such as arts and crafts, sports, games, music, and camping. The specific responsibilities of recreation workers vary greatly with their job title, their level of training, or the state they work in.

Travel Agents (41-3041)

Travel agents sell transportation, lodging, and admission to entertainment activities to individuals and groups who are planning trips. They offer advice on destinations, plan trip itineraries, and make travel arrangements for clients. In addition, resorts and specialty travel groups use travel agents to promote travel packages to their clients.

Waiters and Waitresses (35-3031)

Waiters and waitresses take orders and serve food and beverages to customers in dining establishments. Waiters and waitresses, also called servers, are responsible for ensuring that customers have a satisfying dining experience. The specific duties of servers vary considerably with the establishment in which they work.

10. HUMAN SERVICES

Workers in the human service occupations perform a wide variety of tasks for individuals and the general public. These services may include cutting and styling hair, manicuring, skincare treatments, and fitness training. Some workers provide childcare and animal care, while others clean and care for houses, lawns, and commercial buildings. Services such as these make life easier and more pleasant for people. Another group of more highly trained human service workers aid individual with counseling; providing emotional support; and assistance in dealing with illness, addictions, behavioral problems, and family issues. Upon death of a family member or loved one, funeral directors arrange the details of a funeral. An interest in providing services for the convenience of others and caring about people and wanting to help them are required for human services occupations.

The following occupations are included in the Human Services Career Cluster. For further information about a specific occupation go to *www.bls.gov/ooh/* and key the name of the occupation in the search window.

Animal Care and Service Workers (39-2011, 2021)

Animal care and service workers train, feed, groom, and exercise animals. They also clean, disinfect, and repair the animals' cages. They play with the animals, provide companionship, and observe behavioral changes that could indicate illness or injury. Boarding kennels, pet stores, animal shelters, veterinary hospitals and clinics, stables, laboratories, and zoological parks all house animals and employ animal care and service workers.

Barbers, Hairdressers, and Cosmetologists (39-5011, 5012, 5093)

Barbers, hairdressers, and cosmetologists provide hair styling and beauty services. Barbers cut, trim, shampoo, and style hair, mostly for male clients. Hairdressers, or hairstylists, offer a wide range of hair services, such as shampooing, cutting, coloring, and styling. Cosmetologists provide scalp and facial treatments and makeup analysis. Shampooers wash and rinse customers' hair so a hairstylist can cut and style it.

Childcare Workers (39-9011)

Childcare workers care for children when parents and other family members are unavailable. They care for children's basic needs, such as bathing and feeding. In addition, some help children prepare for kindergarten, and many help older children with homework.

Fitness Trainers and Instructors (39-9031)

Fitness trainers and instructors lead, instruct, and motivate individuals or groups in exercise activities, including cardiovascular exercise (exercises for the heart and blood system), strength training, and stretching. They work with people of all ages and skill levels.

Funeral Directors (39-4831)

Funeral directors, also called morticians and undertakers, manage funeral homes and arrange the details of a funeral. Together with the family, funeral directors establish the locations, dates, and times of wakes, memorial services, and burials. They handle other details as well, such as determining whether the body should be buried, entombed, or cremated.

Grounds Maintenance Workers (37-3010)

Grounds maintenance workers provide a pleasant outdoor environment by ensuring that the grounds of houses, businesses, and parks are attractive, orderly, and healthy. They also care for indoor gardens and plantings in commercial and public facilities, such as malls, hotels, and botanical gardens.

Janitors and Building Cleaners (37-2011)

Janitors and building cleaning workers keep office buildings, schools, hospitals, retail stores, hotels, and other places clean, sanitary, and in good condition. Some do only cleaning, while others have a wide range of duties. Some janitors and building cleaners work outdoors, mowing lawns, sweeping walkways, or shoveling snow. They may also monitor the heating and cooling system, ensuring that it functions properly.

Manicurists and Pedicurists (39-5092)

Manicurists and pedicurists work exclusively on the hands and feet, providing treatments to groom fingernails and toenails. A typical treatment involves soaking the clients' hands or feet to soften the skin to remove dead skin-cells. Manicurists and pedicurists also apply lotion or oil to hands and feet to moisturize the skin. They may also apply, shape, and apply polish to artificial fingernails.

Mental Health Counselors and Marriage and Family Therapists (21-1013, 1014)

Mental health counselors and marriage and family therapists help people manage or overcome mental and emotional disorders and problems with their family and relationships. They listen to clients and ask questions to help the clients understand their problems and develop strategies to improve their lives.

Pest Control Workers (37-2021)

Pest control workers control, manage, or remove unwanted creatures, such as roaches, rats, ants, termites, and bedbugs, that infest buildings and surrounding areas. Unwanted pests that infest buildings or surrounding areas can pose serious risks to the health and safety of occupants. Pest control workers control, manage, or remove these creatures from homes, apartments, offices, and other structures to protect people and to maintain buildings' structural integrity.

Psychologists (19-3030)

Psychology seeks to understand and explain thoughts, emotions, feelings, and behavior. Some psychologists work alone, which may include independent research or individually counseling patients. Others work as part of a healthcare team, collaborating with physicians, social workers, and others to treat illness and promote overall wellness. Many clinical and counseling psychologists in private practice have their own offices and can set their own schedules.

Rehabilitation Counselors (21-1015)

Rehabilitation counselors help people with emotional and physical disabilities live independently. They help their clients overcome personal, social, and professional effects of disabilities as they relate to employment or independent living.

Skincare Specialists (39-5094)

Skincare specialists cleanse and beautify the face and body to enhance a person's appearance. They give facials, full-body treatments, and head and neck massages to improve the health and appearance of the skin. Some may provide other skincare treatments, such as peels, masks, or scrubs, to remove dead or dry skin.

Social and Human Service Assistants (21-1093)

Social and human service assistants help people get through difficult times or get additional support. They help other workers, such as social workers, and they help clients find benefits or community services. Social and human service assistants have many job titles, including case work aide, clinical

Part 2 Exploring Career Clusters

social work aide, family service assistant,
social work assistant, addictions counselor
assistant, and human service worker.

Social Workers (21-1020)

Social workers help people cope with
challenges in every stage of their lives. They
help with a wide range of situations, such as
adopting a child or being diagnosed with a
terminal illness. Social workers work with
many populations, including children, people
with disabilities, and people with addictions.

Substance Abuse and Behavioral Disorder Counselors (21-1011)

Substance abuse and behavioral disorder
counselors advise people who have
alcoholism or other types of addiction, eating
disorders, or other behavioral problems.
They provide treatment and support to help
the client recover from addiction or modify
problem behaviors. They work with clients
both one-on-one and in group sessions.

11. INFORMATION TECHNOLOGY

Information technology products and services are a part of our daily lives and are found in virtually every industry. Almost every company or organization has a computer-related component that is essential to getting the job done. The information technology cluster includes all aspects of managing and processing information and related technologies. Information technology workers are responsible for designing, developing, supporting and managing computer hardware, computer software, information networks, and the Internet. Information technology occupations range from some of the most highly skilled engineers, programmers, and systems analysts to mid-level managers and administrators to computer support specialists.

The following occupations are included in the Information Technology Career Cluster. For further information about a specific occupation go to *www.bls.gov/ooh/* and key the name of the occupation in the search window.

Computer Hardware Engineers (17-2061)

Computer hardware engineers research, design, develop, and test computer equipment such as chips, circuit boards, or routers. By solving complex problems in computer hardware, these engineers create rapid advances in computer technology. Computer hardware engineers ensure that computer hardware components work together with the latest software developments.

Computer and Information Research Scientists (15-1111)

Computer and information research scientists invent and design new technology and find new uses for existing technology. They study and solve complex problems in computing for business, science, medicine, and other uses. In general, computer and information research scientists work on a more theoretical level than other computer professionals.

Computer and Information Systems Managers (11-3021)

Computer and information systems managers, often called information technology managers (IT managers or IT project managers), plan, coordinate, and direct computer-related activities in an organization. They help determine the information technology goals of an organization and are responsible for implementing the appropriate computer systems to meet those goals.

Computer Programmers (15-1131)

Computer programmers write code to create software programs. They turn the program designs created by software developers and engineers into instructions that a computer can follow. Programmers work closely with software developers and, in some businesses, their work overlaps.

Computer Support Specialists (15-1150)

Computer support specialists provide help and advice to people and organizations using computer software or equipment. Some, called technical support specialists, support information technology (IT) employees within their organization. Others, called help-desk technicians, assist non-IT users who are having computer problems.

Computer Systems Analysts (15-1121)

Computer systems analysts study an organization's current computer systems and procedures and make recommendations to management to help the organization operate more efficiently and effectively. They bring business and information technology (IT) together by understanding the needs and limitations of both.

Database Administrators (15-1141)

Database administrators use software to store and organize data, such as financial information and customer shipping records. They make sure that data are available to users and are secure from unauthorized access. Database administrators, often called DBAs, make sure that data analysts can easily use the database to find the information they need and that the system performs as it should.

Desktop Publishers (43-9031)

Desktop publishers use computer software to design page layouts for newspapers, books, brochures, and other items that will be printed or put online. They collect the text, graphics, and other materials they will need and then format them into a finished product. Desktop publishers often work with other design and media professionals, such as writers, editors and graphic designers.

Information Security Analysts, Web Developers, and Computer Network Architects (15-1179)

Information security analysts, web developers, and computer network architects all use information technology (IT) to advance their organization's goals. Security analysts ensure a firm's information stays safe from cyber attacks. Web developers create websites to help firms have a public face. Computer network architects create the internal networks all workers within organizations use.

Network and Computer Systems Administrators (15-1142)

Computer networks are critical parts of almost every organization. Network and computer systems administrators are responsible for the day-to-day operation of these networks. They organize, install, and support an organization's computer systems, including local area networks (LANs), wide area networks (WANs), network segments, intranets, and other data communication systems.

Software Developers (15-1132, 1133)

Software developers are the creative minds behind computer programs. They are in charge of the entire development process for a software program. Some develop the applications that allow people to do specific tasks on a computer or other device. Others develop the underlying systems that run the devices or control networks.

12. LAW, PUBLIC SAFETY, CORRECTIONS, AND SECURITY

This cluster includes occupations concerned with public safety, protective services, legal services, corrections, and related professional and technical support occupations. Law enforcement services workers protect lives and personal property. They maintain order, enforce laws, investigate accidents and crimes, and arrest criminals. Fire and emergency services workers help protect the public against these dangers by responding to a variety of emergencies. Security guards and surveillance officers patrol and protect various public and private properties. Legal services and support workers, primarily lawyers, serve as advocates and advisers for individuals and business. Judges apply the law to court cases and oversee the legal process in courts. Corrections and probation officers supervise individuals who are convicted of a crime or on probation. An interest in safeguarding lives and property, enforcing laws, and using authority to protect people and property is important for protective service workers.

The following occupations are included in the Law, Public Safety, Corrections and Security Career Cluster. For further information about a specific occupation go to *www.bls.gov/ooh/* and key the name of the occupation in the search window.

Correctional Officers (33-3010)

Correctional officers are responsible for overseeing individuals who have been arrested and are awaiting trial or who have been sentenced to serve time in a jail, reformatory, or prison. Inside the prison or jail, correctional officers enforce rules and regulations. They maintain security by preventing any disturbances, assaults, or escapes. Correctional officers supervise the daily activities of inmates, ensuring that inmates obey the rules and finish their work. Correctional officers also ensure that they know where all inmates are.

Court Reporters (23-2091)

Court reporters create word-for-word transcripts of speeches, conversations, legal proceedings, meetings, and other events. They play a critical role in legal proceedings and other meetings where it is important to have a record of exactly what was said. They are responsible for producing a complete, accurate, and secure legal record. Court reporters who work in courts also help judges and trial attorneys by organizing the official record and searching for information in it.

Fire Inspectors and Investigators (33-2021)

Fire inspectors visit and inspect buildings and other structures, such as sports arenas and shopping malls, to search for fire hazards and to ensure that federal, state, and local fire codes are met. They also test and inspect fire protection and fire extinguishing equipment to ensure that it works. Fire investigators determine the origin and cause of fires by searching the surrounding scene and collecting evidence.

Firefighters (33-2011)

Firefighters protect the public by responding to fires and other emergencies. They are frequently the first emergency personnel on the scene of an accident. When responding to an emergency, firefighters do tasks assigned by a superior officer. They might be responsible for connecting hoses to hydrants, operating pumps to power the hoses, climbing ladders, or using tools to break through debris. Other firefighters might be responsible for providing medical attention.

Forensic Science Technicians (19-4092)

Forensic science technicians help investigate crimes by collecting and analyzing physical evidence. Most technicians specialize in either crime scene investigation or

Part 2 Exploring Career Clusters

laboratory analysis. Crime scene investigators may use tweezers, black lights, and specialized kits to identify and collect evidence. In addition to processing crime scenes, they may also attend autopsies.

Judges, Mediators, and Hearing Officers (23-1020)

Judges, mediators, and hearing officers apply the law to court cases and oversee the legal process in courts. They also resolve administrative disputes and facilitate negotiations between opposing parties. Judges preside over trials or hearings. Mediators help opposing parties settle disputes outside of court. Hearing officers usually work for government agencies. They decide many issues, such as if a person is eligible for workers' compensation benefits.

Lawyers (23-1011)

Lawyers advise and represent individuals, businesses, or government agencies on legal issues or disputes. As advocates, they represent one of the parties in criminal and civil trials by presenting evidence and arguing in court to support their client. As advisors, lawyers counsel their clients about their legal rights and obligations and suggest courses of action in business and personal matters. All attorneys research the intent of laws and judicial decisions and apply the laws to the specific circumstances that their clients face.

Paralegals and Legal Assistants (23-2011)

Paralegals and legal assistants do a variety of tasks to support lawyers, including maintaining and organizing files, conducting legal research, and drafting documents. Paralegals and legal assistants help lawyers prepare for hearings, trials, and corporate meetings. However, their specific duties may vary depending on the size of the firm or organization.

Police and Detectives (33-3021, 3031, 3051, 3052)

Police officers protect lives and property. Detectives and criminal investigators, who sometimes are called agents or special agents, gather facts and collect evidence of possible crimes. The daily activities of police and detectives vary with their occupational specialty and whether they are working for a local, state, or federal agency. Duties also differ among federal agencies, which enforce different aspects of the law.

Private Detectives and Investigators (33-9021)

Private detectives and investigators find facts and analyze information about legal, financial, and personal matters. They offer many services, including verifying people's backgrounds, tracing missing persons, investigating computer crimes, and protecting celebrities. Private detectives and investigators typically work for individuals, attorneys, and businesses. Some have their own investigative agency.

Probation Officers and Correctional Treatment Specialists (21-1092)

Many people who are convicted of crimes are placed on probation, instead of being sent to prison. People who have served time in prison are often released on parole. During probation and parole, offenders must stay out of trouble and meet other requirements. Probation officers and correctional treatment specialists work with and monitor offenders to prevent them from committing new crimes.

Security Guards and Gaming Surveillance Officers (33-9031, 9032, 9093)

Security guards and gaming surveillance officers patrol and inspect property against fire, theft, vandalism, terrorism, and illegal activity. They monitor people and buildings in an effort to prevent crime. Guards must remain alert, looking for anything out of the ordinary throughout their shift. In an emergency, guards may call for assistance from police, fire, or ambulance services. Some security guards may be armed.

13. MANUFACTURING

This cluster includes two major groups of occupations: production occupations and mechanical occupations. Automobiles, gasoline, newspapers, eyeglasses, electricity, blue jeans, furniture, and most other products have at least one thing in common: production workers make them. There are hundreds of production occupations, most of which work in manufacturing plants. Production workers perform manual work requiring varying degrees of skill. Some do little more than start and stop a machine, and watch it while it is running. Others do highly skilled work requiring a great deal of precision.

Eventually all machines and equipment with mechanical and electrical parts require service or repair. Mechanical workers install, service, and repair various types of machines and equipment. Mechanics, installers, and repairers work in all industries. The largest proportions of such workers are employed in manufacturing plants that produce steel, automobiles, aircraft, and other durable goods. About an equal number of workers are employed in retail trade. These firms sell and service automobiles, household appliances, farm implements, and other mechanical equipment. Mechanical workers often work alone and set their own schedule, but they have to get the work done correctly and on time.

The following occupations are included in the Manufacturing Career Cluster. For further information about a specific occupation go to *www.bls.gov/ooh/* and key the name of the occupation in the search window.

Aircraft and Avionics Equipment Mechanics and Technicians (49-2091, 3011)

Aircraft and avionics equipment mechanics and technicians repair and perform scheduled maintenance on airplanes and helicopters. They also inspect airplanes and helicopters as required by the Federal Aviation Administration (FAA).

Assemblers and Fabricators (51-2000)

Assemblers and fabricators have an important role in the manufacturing process. They assemble both finished products and the pieces that go into them. The products encompass a full range of manufactured products, including aircraft, toys, household appliances, automobiles, computers, and electronic devices.

Automotive Body and Glass Repairers (49-3021, 3022)

Automotive body and glass repairers restore, refinish, and replace vehicle bodies and frames, windshields, and window glass. They can repair most damage from everyday vehicle collisions and make vehicles look and drive like new. Damage may be minor, such as replacing a cracked windshield, or major, such as replacing an entire door panel.

Automotive Service Technicians and Mechanics (49-3023)

Automotive service technicians and mechanics, often called service technicians or service techs, inspect, maintain, and repair cars and light trucks. Service technicians work on traditional mechanical components, such as engines, transmissions, belts, and hoses. However, they must also be familiar with a growing number of electronic systems. Braking, transmission, and steering systems, for example, are controlled primarily by computers and electronic components.

Bakers (51-3011)

Bakers mix and bake ingredients according to recipes to make a variety of breads, pastries, and other baked goods. Commercial bakers are commonly employed in manufacturing facilities that produce breads and pastries. Retail bakers work primarily in grocery stores and specialty shops, including bakeries. Some retail bakers own bakery shops or other types of businesses where they make baked goods.

Computer, ATM, and Office Machine Repairers (49-2011)

Computer, ATM, and office machine repairers install, fix, and maintain many of the machines that businesses, households, and other consumers use. In most cases, machines do not break down entirely. Often just one broken part can keep a machine from working properly. Repairers often fix machines by replacing these parts and other defective equipment.

Dental Laboratory Technicians (51-9081)

Dental laboratory technicians use impressions, or molds, of a patient's teeth to create crowns, bridges, dentures, and other dental appliances. They work closely with dentists but have limited contact with patients. In small laboratories, technicians do all stages of the work. In large laboratories, technicians may work on only one step of the process, such as waxing or polishing appliances.

Diesel Service Technicians and Mechanics (49-3031)

Diesel service technicians and mechanics inspect, repair, or overhaul buses and trucks engines. Other heavy vehicles and mobile equipment, including bulldozers and cranes, also are powered by diesel engines, as are many commercial boats, passenger vehicles, pickups, and other work trucks. Diesel service technicians who service and repair these engines are commonly known as diesel mechanics.

Electrical and Electronics Installers and Repairers (49-2090)

Electrical and electronics installers and repairers install, repair, or replace a variety of electrical equipment in telecommunications, transportation, utilities, and other industries. Automated electronic control systems are becoming increasingly complex. As a result, repairers use software programs and testing equipment to diagnose malfunctions.

Food Processing Occupations (51-3021, 3022, 3091)

Food processing occupations include butchers and meat cutters; meat, poultry, and fish cutters and trimmers; and operators and tenders of roasting, baking, and drying machinery. These workers cut, trim, or otherwise process food items, such as meat, or nonfood items, such as tobacco, for retail sale.

Food Processing Operators (51-3092, 3093)

Food processing operators include food batch makers and food cooking machine operators and tenders. These workers may set up, operate, and tend cooking equipment that mixes, blends, cooks, or otherwise processes ingredients used to manufacture food products.

General Maintenance and Repair Workers (49-9071)

General maintenance and repair workers maintain and repair machines, mechanical equipment, and buildings. They work on plumbing, electrical, and air-conditioning and heating systems. They are hired for maintenance and repair tasks that are not complex enough to need the specialized training of a licensed tradesperson, such as a plumber or electrician.

Heating, Air Conditioning, and Refrigeration Mechanics and Installers (49-9021)

Heating, air conditioning, and refrigeration mechanics and installers—often referred to as HVACR technicians—work on heating, ventilation, cooling, and refrigeration systems that control the air quality in many types of buildings. Although trained to do all three, HVACR technicians sometimes work strictly with heating, air-conditioning, or refrigeration systems.

Heavy Vehicle and Mobile Equipment Service Technicians (49-3040)

Heavy vehicle and mobile equipment service technicians inspect, maintain, and repair vehicles and machinery used in construction, farming, rail transportation, and other industries. They repair and maintain engines, hydraulic systems, transmissions, and electrical systems. With many types of equipment and mechanical and electrical systems, service technicians use diagnostic computers to identify problems and make adjustments or repairs.

Home Appliance Repairers (49-9031)

Home appliance repairers install and repair household appliances, such as refrigerators, microwaves, and washer and dryers. Home appliance repairers, often called home appliance repair technicians, usually travel to customers' homes to do their work. After identifying problems, workers repair or replace defective belts, motors, heating elements, switches, gears, or other items. They also may tighten, align, clean, and lubricate parts as necessary.

Home Entertainment Equipment Installers and Repairers (49-2097)

Home entertainment equipment installers and repairers, also called service technicians, set up and fix household audio and video equipment, such as televisions, stereo components, and home theater systems. They install, troubleshoot, and fine-tune sound and picture quality, ensuring that a client's home entertainment system works at its peak capability.

Industrial Machinery Mechanics and Maintenance Workers (49-9041, 4043)

Industrial machinery mechanics and maintenance workers maintain and repair factory equipment and other industrial machinery, such as conveying systems, production machinery, and packaging equipment. Industrial machinery mechanics keep machines in good working order.

Machinery maintenance workers do basic maintenance and repairs on machines.

Industrial Production Managers (11-3051)

Industrial production managers oversee the daily operations of manufacturing and related plants. They coordinate, plan, and direct the activities used to create a wide range of goods, such as cars, computer equipment, or paper products. Depending on the size of the manufacturing plant, industrial production managers may oversee the entire plant or just one area of it.

Jewelers and Precious Stone and Metal Workers (51-9071)

Jewelers and precious stone and metal workers design, manufacture, and sell jewelry. They also adjust, repair, and appraise gems and jewelry. Jewelers and precious stone and metal workers usually specialize in one of four specific occupations: precious metal worker, gemologist, jewelry appraiser, or bench jeweler.

Laundry and Dry-cleaning Workers (51-6011)

Laundry and dry-cleaning workers clean clothing, linens, drapes, and other articles, using washing, drying, and dry-cleaning machines. They also may clean leather, suede, furs, and rugs. When necessary, workers treat spots and stains on articles before washing or dry-cleaning. They monitor machines during the cleaning process and ensure that items are not lost or placed with items of another customer.

Line Installers and Repairers (49-9051, 9052)

Every time you turn on your lights, call someone on the phone, watch cable television, or access the Internet, you are connecting to complex networks of physical power lines and cables that provide you with electricity and connect you with the outside world. Line installers and repairers, also known as line workers or linemen, are the people who install and maintain these networks.

Machinists and Tool and Die Makers (51-4041, 4043)

Machinists and tool and die makers set up and operate a variety of machine tools. Machinists use machine tools that are either conventionally controlled or computer numerically controlled, such as lathes, milling machines, and grinders, to produce precision metal parts. Toolmakers construct precision tools and tool holders that are used to cut, shape, and form metal and other materials Die makers construct metal forms, called dies, which are used to shape metal in stamping and forging operations.

Medical Appliance Technicians (51-9082)

Medical appliance technicians construct, fit, and repair medical supportive devices, including prosthetic limbs, arch supports, facial parts, and foot and leg braces. They use many different types of materials, such as metal, plastic, and leather, to create a variety of medical devices for patients who need them because of a birth defect, an accident, disease, amputation, or the effects of aging.

Medical Equipment Repairers (49-9062)

Medical equipment repairers, also known as biomedical equipment technicians (BMET), repair a wide variety of electronic, electromechanical, and hydraulic equipment used in hospitals and health practitioners' offices. They may work on patient monitors, defibrillators, medical imaging equipment (X rays, CAT scanners, and ultrasound equipment), voice-controlled operating tables, and electric wheelchairs, as well as on sophisticated medical equipment that dentists and eye doctors use.

Metal and Plastic Machine Workers (51-4000)

Metal and plastic machine workers set up and operate machines that cut, shape, and form metal and plastic materials or pieces. Metal and plastic machine workers are employed mainly in factories. In general, these workers are separated into two groups: those who set up machines for operation and those who operate machines during production.

Millwrights (49-9044)

Millwrights are highly skilled workers. Putting together a machine can take a few days or several weeks. Millwrights need to have a good understanding of how the machine works so that they can repair it when it breaks down. Repair includes replacing, as needed, worn or defective parts of the machinery.

Ophthalmic Laboratory Technicians (51-9083)

Ophthalmic laboratory technicians make prescription eyeglasses and contact lenses. They are also commonly known as manufacturing opticians, optical mechanics, or optical goods workers. Although they make some lenses by hand, technicians often use automated equipment. Some technicians manufacture lenses for other optical instruments, such as telescopes and binoculars.

Painting and Coating Workers (51-9121, 9122, 9123)

Painting and coating workers paint and coat a wide range of products, including cars, jewelry, lacquer, and candy. Workers may use a number of techniques to apply the paint or coating. Perhaps the most straightforward technique is dipping an item in a large vat of paint or some other coating. Spraying products with a solution of paint or another coating is also common. Some factories use automated painting systems.

Power Plant Operators, Distributors, and Dispatchers (51-8010)

Electricity is generated from many sources, including coal, gas, nuclear energy, hydroelectric energy (from water sources), and wind and solar power. Power plant operators, distributors, and dispatchers control power plants and the flow of electricity from plants to substations, which distribute electricity to businesses, homes, and factories.

Printing Workers (51-5100)

Printing workers produce print material in three stages: prepress, press, and binding and finishing. They review specifications, identify and fix problems with printing equipment, and assemble pages. In small print shops, the same person may take care of all three stages. However, in most print shops, workers specialize in one of the three stages.

Quality Control Inspectors (51-9061)

Quality control inspectors examine products and materials for defects or deviations from manufacturers' or industry specifications. Quality control inspectors ensure that your food will not make you sick, that your car will run properly, and that your pants will not split the first time you wear them. These workers monitor quality standards for nearly all manufactured products, including foods, textiles, clothing, glassware, motor vehicles, electronic components, computers, and structural steel.

Semiconductor Processors (51-9141)

Semiconductor processors oversee the manufacturing of electronic semiconductors, which are commonly known as integrated circuits or microchips. These microchips are found in all electronic devices and are an important part of modern life. Processors are largely responsible for quality control in the manufacturing process. They check equipment regularly for problems and test completed chips to make sure they work properly.

Sewers and Tailors (51-6050)

Sewers and tailors sew, join, reinforce, or finish clothing or other items. They may create new pieces of clothing from patterns and designs or alter existing garments to fit customers better. Those who do alterations ensure that clothes fit customers properly.

They make changes to garments, such as hemming pants to make them shorter or taking in seams to make clothing smaller.

Slaughterers and Meat Packers (51-3023)

Slaughterers and meat packers kill and clean animals, divide carcasses into manageable sections, and grind or otherwise prepare and pack products, such as boxed beef, for shipping to distribution centers. Slaughterers and meat packers typically work in either slaughtering yards or processing facilities. They may be rotated through stations, doing different tasks each shift.

Small Engine Mechanics (49-3050)

Small engine mechanics inspect, service, and repair motorized power equipment. Mechanics often specialize in one type of equipment, such as motorcycles, motorboats, or outdoor power equipment. When equipment breaks down, mechanics use many strategies to diagnose the source and the extent of the problem. Small engine mechanics determine mechanical, electrical, and fuel problems and make necessary repairs.

Stationary Engineers and Boiler Operators (51-8021)

Stationary engineers and boiler operators control stationary engines, boilers, or other mechanical equipment to provide utilities for buildings or for industrial purposes. They start up, regulate, repair, and shut down equipment. They monitor meters, gauges, and computerized controls to ensure that equipment operates safely and within established limits. They use sophisticated electrical and electronic test equipment when servicing, troubleshooting, repairing, and monitoring heating, cooling, and ventilation systems.

Telecommunications Equipment Installers and Repairers Except Line Installers (49-2022)

Telephone, computer, and cable telecommunications systems rely on sophisticated equipment to process and transmit vast amounts of information. Telecommunications equipment installers and repairers, also known as telecom technicians, set up and maintain devices or equipment that carry communications signals, connect to telephone lines, or access the Internet.

Upholsterers (51-6093)

Upholsterers make, replace, and repair coverings on furniture and in vehicles. Upholsterers put on covering and cushions to create new furniture and update old furniture and vehicle interiors. Although some upholsterers specialize in either working with old furniture or creating new furniture, most do both.

Water and Wastewater Treatment Plant and System Operators (51-8031)

Water and wastewater treatment plant and system operators manage a system of machines, often through the use of control boards, to transfer or treat water or wastewater. The specific duties of plant operators depend on the type and size of the plant. In a small plant, one operator may be responsible for maintaining all of the systems. In large plants, multiple operators work the same shifts and are more specialized in their duties, often relying on computerized systems to help them monitor plant processes.

Welders, Cutters, Solderers, and Brazers (51-4121)

Welders, cutters, solderers, and brazers weld or join metal parts. They also fill holes, indentions, or seams of metal products, using hand-held welding equipment. Welders work in a wide variety of industries, from car racing to manufacturing. Cutters use heat to cut and trim metal objects to specific dimensions. Solderers and brazers also use heat to join two or more metal items together.

Woodworkers (51-7000)

Woodworkers build a variety of products, such as cabinets and furniture, using wood. Many of these products are mass produced, including most furniture, kitchen cabinets, and musical instruments. Other products are custom made with specialized tools in small shops. The modern woodworking trade is highly technical and relies on advanced equipment and highly skilled operators. Workers use automated machinery, such as computerized numerical control (CNC) machines, to do much of the work.

14. MARKETING, SALES, AND SERVICE

Whenever you buy a product or a service, you benefit from the work of someone in marketing, sales, and service. The most familiar sales and service workers are the retail salespersons, cashiers, and customer service representatives that work at dozens of different types of large and small retail stores. These include department, discount, electronic, hardware, building materials, carpet, appliance and others. The people you are less likely to come in contact with are market research analysts, buyers and purchasing agents, sales representatives, and advertising and marketing managers who are responsible for planning, acquiring, promoting, and presenting goods for consumers to purchase. Other workers in this cluster include real estate and insurance sales agents. Personal attributes are more important in marketing and sales than in most other occupations. Sales workers must be outgoing, enthusiastic, and persuasive.

The following occupations are included in the Marketing, Sales and Service Career Cluster. For further information about a specific occupation go to *www.bls. gov/ooh/* and key the name of the occupation in the search window.

Advertising Sales Agents (41-3011)

Advertising sales agents, also called account executives and advertising sales representatives, sell advertising space to businesses and individuals. They contact potential clients, make sales presentations, and maintain client accounts. Most advertising sales agents work outside the office occasionally, calling on clients and prospective clients at their places of business.

Advertising, Promotions, and Marketing Managers (11-2011, 2021)

Advertising, promotions, and marketing managers plan programs to generate interest in a product or service. They work with art directors, sales agents, and financial staff members. Often, advertising managers serve as liaisons between the client requiring the advertising and an advertising or promotion agency that develops and places the ads.

Cashiers (41-2011)

Cashiers handle payments from customers purchasing goods and services. Most cashiers work in retail establishments such as supermarkets, department stores, movie theaters, and restaurants. The work is often repetitive, and cashiers spend most of their time standing behind counters or checkout stands.

Customer Service Representatives (43-4051)

Customer service representatives interact with customers on behalf of an organization. They provide information about products and services and respond to customer complaints. Some also take orders and process returns. Many customer service representatives answer incoming calls in telephone call centers, which are increasingly called customer contact centers.

Demonstrators and Product Promoters (41-9011)

Demonstrators and product promoters create public interest in products, such as cosmetics, house wares, and food. They encourage people and stores to buy their products by showing the products to prospective customers and answering questions. They attract potential customers by offering samples, holding contests, or distributing prizes.

Part 2 Exploring Career Clusters

Insurance Sales Agents (41-3021)

Insurance sales agents help insurance companies generate new business by contacting potential customers and selling one or more types of insurance. An agent explains various insurance policies and helps clients choose plans that suit them. Insurance sales agents commonly sell one or more types of insurance, such as property and casualty, life, and health and long-term care.

Market Research Analysts (13-1161)

Market research analysts perform research and gather data to help a company market its products or services. They study market conditions in local, regional, or national areas to examine potential sales of a product or service. They help companies understand what products people want, who will buy them, and at what price.

Models (41-9012)

Models pose for artists, photographers, or customers to help advertise a variety of products, including clothing, cosmetics, food, and appliances. Almost all models work with agents, who provide a link between the models and clients. Models spend a considerable amount of time promoting themselves by putting together and maintaining portfolios, printing composite cards, and traveling to meet potential clients.

Purchasing Managers, Buyers, and Purchasing Agents (13-1020)

Purchasing managers, buyers, and purchasing agents buy products for organizations to use or resell. They evaluate suppliers, negotiate contracts, and review product quality. They consider price, quality, availability, reliability, and technical support when choosing suppliers and merchandise. To be effective, they must have a working technical knowledge of the goods or services to be bought.

Real Estate Brokers and Sales Agents (41-9020)

Real estate brokers and sales agents help clients buy, sell, and rent properties. Brokers and agents do the same type of work, but brokers are licensed to manage their own real estate businesses. Sales agents must work with a broker. Although most real estate brokers and sales agents sell residential property, others sell commercial property, and a small number sell industrial, agricultural, or other types of real estate.

Retail Sales Workers (41-2022, 2031)

Retail sales workers include both those who sell retail merchandise, such as clothing, furniture, and automobiles, (called retail salespersons) and those who sell spare and replacement parts and equipment, especially car parts, (called parts salespersons). Both groups help customers find the products they want and process customers' payments.

Sales Engineers (41-9031)

Sales engineers sell complex scientific and technological products or services to businesses. They must have extensive knowledge of the products' parts and functions and must understand the scientific processes that make these products work. Some sales engineers work for the companies that design and build technical products. Others work for independent sales firms.

Sales Managers (11-2022)

Sales managers direct organizations' sales teams. They set sales goals, analyze data, and develop training programs for the organization's sales representatives. Most sales managers direct the distribution of goods and services by assigning sales territories, setting sales goals, and establishing training programs for the organization's sales representatives.

Wholesale and Manufacturing Sales Representatives (41-4011, 4012)

Wholesale and manufacturing sales representatives, sometimes called manufacturers' representatives or manufacturers' agents, sell goods for wholesalers or manufacturers to businesses, government agencies, and other organizations. They contact customers, explain product features, answer any questions that their customers may have, and negotiate prices.

15. SCIENCE, TECHNOLOGY, ENGINEERING, AND MATHEMATICS

This cluster includes occupations in three major groups: natural science and mathematics, engineering, and technologists and technicians. Engineers apply the principles of science and mathematics to develop economical solutions to technical problems. Their work is the link between scientific discoveries and the commercial applications that meet societal and consumer demands. Most engineers specialize in such fields as aerospace, chemical engineering, electrical engineering, industrial engineering, and more than a dozen other specialties. Natural and mathematical scientists seek knowledge of the physical world through observation, study, and experimentation. The knowledge gained through these research activities is used to develop new products, increase productivity, protect the environment, and improve health care. Technologists and technicians perform much of the detailed work necessary in engineering and science. They perform the day-to-day tasks needed to carry out a project or run an operation. They are usually part of a team that is engaged in a particular project or operation.

The following occupations are included in the Science, Technology, Engineering and Mathematics Career Cluster. For further information about a specific occupation go to *www.bls.gov/ooh/* and key the name of the occupation in the search window.

Actuaries (15-2011)

Actuaries analyze the financial costs of risk and uncertainty. They use mathematics, statistics, and financial theory to assess the risk that an event will occur and to help businesses and clients develop policies that minimize the cost of that risk.

Aerospace Engineering and Operations Technicians (17-3021)

Aerospace engineering and operations technicians operate and maintain equipment used in developing, testing, and producing new aircraft and spacecraft. Increasingly, they use computer-based modeling and simulation tools and processes in this work.

Aerospace Engineers (17-2011)

Aerospace engineers design aircraft, spacecraft, satellites, and missiles. Aerospace engineers may develop new technologies for use in aviation, defense systems, and spacecraft. In addition, they test prototypes to make sure that they function according to design.

Architectural and Engineering Managers (11-9041)

Architectural and engineering managers plan, coordinate, and direct activities in architecture and engineering, including research and development in these fields. They determine technical goals, such as improving manufacturing or building processes, or developing new products or designs, and then they make detailed plans to accomplish these goals.

Anthropologists and Archeologists (19-3091)

Anthropologists and archeologists study the origin, development, and behavior of human beings, past and present. They examine the cultures, languages, archeological remains, and physical characteristics of people in various parts of the world.

Biochemists and Biophysicists (19-1021)

Biochemists and biophysicists study the chemical and physical principles of living things and of biological processes such as cell development, growth, and heredity. They use advanced technologies to conduct scientific experiments and analysis. For example, they use computer modeling software to determine the three-dimensional structures of proteins and other molecules.

Biological Technicians (19-4021)

Biological technicians help biological and medical scientists conduct laboratory tests and experiments. Most biological technicians work on teams. Typically, technicians are responsible for doing scientific tests, experiments, and analyses under the supervision of biologists or other scientists who direct and evaluate their work.

Biomedical Engineers (17-2031)

Biomedical engineers analyze and design solutions to problems in biology and medicine, with the goal of improving the quality and effectiveness of patient care. Biomedical engineers may design instruments, devices, and software; bring together knowledge from many technical sources to develop new procedures; or conduct research needed to solve clinical problems.

Chemical Engineers (17-2041)

Chemical engineers apply the principles of chemistry, biology, and physics to solve problems. These problems involve the production or use of chemicals, fuel, drugs, food, and many other products. They design processes and equipment for large-scale safe and sustainable manufacturing, plan and test methods of manufacturing products and treating byproducts, and supervise production.

Chemical Technicians (19-4031)

Chemical technicians use special instruments and techniques to help chemists and chemical engineers in researching, developing, and producing chemical products and processes. Most chemical technicians work on teams. Typically, they are supervised by chemists or chemical engineers who direct their work and evaluate their results.

Chemists and Materials Scientists (19-2031, 2032)

Chemists and materials scientists study the structures, compositions, reactions, and other properties of substances. They use their knowledge to develop new and improved products, processes, and materials. Many chemists and materials scientists work in basic and applied research.

Electrical and Electronic Engineering Technicians (17-3023)

Electrical and electronic engineering technicians help engineers design and develop computers, communications equipment, medical monitoring devices, navigational equipment, and other electrical and electronic equipment. They often work in product evaluation and testing, using measuring and diagnostic devices to adjust, test, and repair equipment.

Electrical and Electronics Engineers (17-2071, 2072)

Electrical engineers design, develop, test, and supervise the manufacturing of electrical equipment such as electric motors, radar and navigation systems, communications systems, and power generation equipment. Electronics engineers design and develop electronic equipment, such as broadcast and communications systems—from portable music players to global positioning systems (GPS).

Electro-mechanical Technicians (17-3024)

Electro-mechanical technicians combine knowledge of mechanical technology with knowledge of electrical and electronic circuits. They install, troubleshoot, repair, and upgrade electronic and computer-controlled mechanical systems, such as robotic assembly machines.

Health and Safety Engineers (17-2111)

Health and safety engineers develop procedures and design systems to keep people from getting sick or injured and to keep property from being damaged. They combine knowledge of health or safety and of systems engineering to make sure that chemicals, machinery, software, furniture, and other products are not going to cause harm to people or buildings.

Industrial Engineering Technicians (17-3026)

Industrial engineering technicians plan ways to effectively use personnel, materials, and machines in factories, stores, hospitals, repair shops, and offices. As assistants to industrial engineers, they help prepare machinery and equipment layouts, plan workflows, conduct statistical production studies, and analyze production costs.

Industrial Engineers (17-2112)

Industrial engineers find ways to eliminate wastefulness in production processes. They devise efficient ways to use workers, machines, materials, information, and energy to make a product or provide a service. Industrial engineers apply their skills to many different situations from manufacturing to business administration.

Marine Engineers and Naval Architects (17-2121)

Marine engineers and naval architects design, build, and maintain ships from aircraft carriers to submarines, from sailboats to tankers. Marine engineers work on the mechanical systems, such as propulsion and steering. Naval architects work on the basic design, including the form and stability of hulls.

Materials Engineers (17-2131)

Materials engineers develop, process, and test materials used to create a range of products, from computer chips and aircraft wings to golf clubs and snow skis. They work with metals, ceramics, semiconductors, plastics, composites, and other substances to create new materials that meet certain mechanical, electrical, and chemical requirements. They also develop new ways to use materials.

Mathematicians (15-2021)

Mathematicians use high-level mathematics and technology to develop new mathematical principles, understand relationships between existing principles, and solve real-world problems. Applied mathematicians use theories and techniques, such as mathematical modeling, to solve practical problems. Theoretical mathematicians identify unexplained issues and seek to resolve them.

Mechanical Engineers (17-2141)

Mechanical engineering is one of the broadest engineering disciplines. Mechanical engineers design, develop, build, and test mechanical devices. They use many types of tools, engines, and machines such as power producing machines, power using machines, and industrial production equipment.

Mechanical Engineering Technicians (17-3027)

Mechanical engineering technicians help mechanical engineers design, develop, test, and manufacture industrial machinery, consumer products, and other equipment. They may make sketches and rough layouts, record and analyze data, make calculations and estimates, and report their findings.

Microbiologists (19-1022)

Microbiologists study the growth, development, and other characteristics of microscopic organisms such as bacteria, algae, and fungi. Most microbiologists work in research and development. Many conduct basic research with the aim of increasing scientific knowledge. Others conduct applied research, using knowledge from basic research to develop new products or solve particular problems.

Natural Sciences Managers (11-9121)

Natural sciences managers supervise the work of scientists, including chemists, physicists, and biologists. They direct research and development projects and coordinate activities such as testing, quality control, and production. During all stages of a project, natural sciences managers spend a lot of time coordinating the activities of their unit with those of other units or organizations.

Nuclear Engineers (17-2161)

Nuclear engineers research and develop the processes, instruments, and systems used to get benefits from nuclear energy and radiation. Many of these engineers find industrial and medical uses for radioactive materials—for example, in equipment used in medical diagnosis and treatment.

Nuclear Technicians (19-4051)

Nuclear technicians assist physicists, engineers, and other professionals in nuclear research and nuclear production. They operate special equipment used in these activities and monitor the levels of radiation that are produced. Most nuclear technicians work in nuclear power plants, where they ensure that reactors and other equipment are operated safely and efficiently.

Operations Research Analysts (15-2031)

Operations research analysts use advanced methods of analysis to help organizations solve problems and make better decisions. Operations research analysts are involved in all aspects of an organization. For example, they help allocate resources, develop production schedules, manage the supply chain, and set prices.

Physicists and Astronomers (19-2011, 2012)

Physicists and astronomers study the fundamental nature of the universe, ranging from the vastness of space to the smallest of subatomic particles. They develop new technologies, methods, and theories based on the results of their research that deepen our understanding of how things work and contribute to innovative, real-world applications.

Statisticians (15-2041)

Statisticians use mathematical techniques to analyze and interpret data and draw conclusions. Statisticians design surveys, experiments, and opinion polls to collect data. Statisticians work in many fields, such as education, marketing, psychology, and sports: any field that requires collection and analysis of large amounts of data. In particular, government, health, and manufacturing employ many statisticians.

16. TRANSPORTATION, DISTRIBUTION, AND LOGISTICS

The majority of workers in transportation occupations operate transportation equipment such as taxicabs, limousines, trucks, buses, planes, trains, and ships. Others operate industrial moving equipment such as cranes, power shovels, graders, and industrial trucks. Although these occupations are found in all industries, they are concentrated in the transportation industry. Other workers such as cargo and freight agents provide professional and support services, and some, like flight attendants, provide personal services to passengers. Many others move freight, stock, or other materials around storage facilities or pack materials for moving.

The following occupations are included in the Transportation, Distribution and Logistics Career Cluster. For further information about a specific occupation go to *www.bls.gov/ooh/* and key the name of the occupation in the search window.

Air Traffic Controllers (53-2021)

Air traffic controllers coordinate the movement of air traffic to ensure that planes stay safe distances apart. They manage the flow of airplanes in and out of the airport, guide pilots during takeoff and landing, and monitor airplanes as they travel through the skies.

Airline and Commercial Pilots (53-2011, 2012)

Airline and commercial pilots fly and navigate airplanes or helicopters. Airline pilots fly for airlines that transport people and cargo on a fixed schedule. Commercial pilots fly aircraft for other reasons, such as charter flights, rescue operations, firefighting, aerial photography, and crop dusting.

Bus Drivers (53-3021, 3022)

Bus drivers transport people between a variety of places including work, school, shopping, and across state borders. Some drive regular routes, and others transport passengers on chartered trips or sightseeing tours.

Cargo and Freight Agents (43-5011)

Cargo and freight agents facilitate shipments of goods through airline, train, and trucking terminals and shipping docks. Agents ensure that shipments are picked up and delivered on time, paperwork is completed, and fees are collected. For international shipments, agents prepare and verify customs and tariff forms.

Couriers and Messengers (43-5021)

Couriers and messengers transport documents and packages for individuals, businesses, institutions, and government agencies. Couriers and messengers provide door-to-door delivery service for a variety of clients, including law offices, banks, and hospitals. Most workers specialize in local deliveries, often in large urban areas.

Delivery Truck Drivers and Driver/Sales Workers (53-3031, 3033)

Delivery truck drivers and driver/sales workers pick up, transport, and drop off packages within a small region or urban area. Most of the time, they transport merchandise from a distribution center to businesses and households.

Flight Attendants (53-2031)

Airline companies are required by law to provide flight attendants for the safety and security of passengers. The primary job of flight attendants is to keep passengers safe and to ensure that everyone follows security regulations. Flight attendants also try to make flights comfortable and enjoyable for passengers.

Hand Laborers and Material Movers
(53-7060, 7081)

Hand laborers and material movers transport objects without using machines. Some workers move freight, stock, or other materials around storage facilities; others clean vehicles; some pick up unwanted household goods; and still others pack materials for moving.

Heavy and Tractor-trailer Truck Drivers
(53-3032)

Heavy and tractor-trailer truck drivers transport goods from one location to another. Most tractor-trailer drivers are long-haul drivers and operate trucks with a capacity of at least 26,001 pounds per gross vehicle weight (GVW). They deliver goods over intercity routes, sometimes spanning several states.

Logisticians (13-1081)

Logisticians analyze and coordinate an organization's supply chain—the system that moves a product from supplier to consumer. They manage the entire life cycle of a product, which includes how a product is acquired, distributed, allocated, and delivered.

Material Moving Machine Operators
(53-7000)

Material moving machine operators use machinery to transport various objects. Some operators move construction materials around building sites or earth around a mine. Others move goods around a warehouse or onto and off container ships.

Material Recording Clerks
(43-5061, 5071, 5081, 5111)

Material recording clerks keep track of information to keep businesses and supply chains on schedule. They ensure proper scheduling, recordkeeping, and inventory control. Many clerks use tablets or hand-held computers to keep track of inventory.

New sensors and tags enable these computers to automatically detect when and where products are moved, making clerks' jobs more efficient.

Railroad Conductors and Yardmasters
(53-4031)

Conductors travel on both freight and passenger trains. They coordinate activities of the train crew. On passenger trains, they ensure safety and comfort and make announcements to keep passengers informed. On freight trains, they oversee, and are ultimately responsible for, the loading and unloading of cargo. Yardmasters do work similar to that of conductors, except that they do not travel on trains.

Subway and Streetcar Operators (53-4041)

Subway and streetcar operators transport passengers in urban and suburban areas. Subway operators drive trains that run on separate tracks that may be underground or above ground. Streetcar operators drive electric-powered streetcars, trolleys, and light-rail vehicles that run on streets or on separate tracks above ground.

Taxi Drivers and Chauffeurs (53-3041)

Taxi drivers and chauffeurs drive people to and from the places they need to go, such as homes, workplaces, airports, and shopping centers. They must know their way around a city to take both residents and visitors to their destinations.

Train Engineers and Operators
(53-4010, 4021)

Train engineers and train operators ensure that freight trains and passenger trains stay on time and travel safely. Train engineers drive trains. Train operators work the brakes, signals, or switches. Train engineers and operators check the mechanical condition of locomotives and make adjustments when necessary, document issues with a train that require further inspection, and operate locomotive engines within or between stations.

Water Transportation Occupations
(53-5010, 5020, 5030)

Workers in water transportation occupations operate and maintain ships that take cargo and people over water. These ships travel to and from foreign ports across the ocean, to domestic ports along the coasts, across the Great Lakes, and along the country's many inland waterways.

OCCUPATIONAL SEARCH FORM

TITLE OF THE OCCUPATION ___________________________

A. WHAT WORKERS DO

Give the definition of the occupation. ___________________________

____

____

____

List five major duties of the occupation.

1. ___________________________

   ____

2. ___________________________

   ____

3. ___________________________

   ____

4. ___________________________

   ____

5. ___________________________

   ____

B. WORK ENVIRONMENT

Number of jobs in the occupation _______________ Year provided _______________

In what types of industries or locations do people work? _______________

____

____

____

____

Write down the normal work schedule, if provided. _______________

____

____

____

____

Describe the typical working conditions. ____

____

____

Are there unpleasant or dangerous aspects to this occupation? _________________________

____

____

C. HOW TO BECOME ONE (Education & Training, Qualification, Advancement)

What is the preferred or required level of education or training? ________________________

____

List any licensure or certification requirements. _____________________________________

____

List any special abilities or qualifications recommended or required. __________________

____

____

What opportunities are there for advancement? ______________________________________

____

____

D. PAY

Median annual or hourly wage ____________________ Year provided ____________________

Earnings: top 10% ____________________ Earnings: bottom 10% ____________________

Is this occupation ABOVE or BELOW average for all occupations? ______________________

E. JOB OUTLOOK

What is the expected change in employment for this occupation, 20__/20__? ____________

Describe the future job prospects for this occupation. ________________________________

____

____

____

____

F. SIMILAR OCCUPATIONS

List four to six occupations with similar duties. _____________________________________

____

____

____

Which edition of the Occupational Outlook Handbook did you use for this information?   20__/20__